WORKBOOK

WORKING WITH GRAMMAR

HOW TO BREAK IT DOWN & MAKE IT WORK FOR YOU!

WORKBOOK

WORKING WITH GRAMMAR

HOW TO BREAK IT DOWN & MAKE IT WORK FOR YOU!

Published by
Heron Books, Inc.
20950 SW Rock Creek Road
Sheridan, OR 97378

heronbooks.com

Special thanks to all the teachers and students who
provided feedback instrumental to this edition.

Second Edition © 2004, 2023 Heron Books
All Rights Reserved

ISBN: 978-0-89739-118-4

The Heron Books name and the heron bird symbol are registered trademarks
of Delphi Schools, Inc.

Any unauthorized copying, translation, duplication or distribution, in whole or in part, by any means,
including electronic copying, storage or transmission, is a violation of applicable laws.

Printed in the USA

20 August 2023

CONTENTS

PART 1
NOUNS AND PRONOUNS

Grammar? 3
Sentences & Parts of Speech 4
Nouns 5
Pronouns 9

PART 2
VERBS

Verbs 35
Transitive And Intransitive Verbs 41
Subject-Verb Agreement 48
The Four Forms Of Verbs 50
Verb Tenses 54

PART 3
OTHER PARTS OF SPEECH

Adjectives 65
Adverbs 70
Comparison 75
Modifiers Made From Verbs 77

Prepositions 84

Conjunctions 92

Interjections 97

The Eight Parts Of Speech 98

PART 4
THE SENTENCE

The Sentence 103

Clauses 105

Sentence Errors 111

Three Ways To Build Sentences 115

PART 5
JOBS NOUNS AND PRONOUNS DO IN SENTENCES

Jobs Nouns And Pronouns Do In Sentences 123

Direct Objects 126

Indirect Objects 129

The Object Of A Preposition 132

The Noun Restatement 135

Verbs Can Act As Nouns 139

PART 6
WHAT IS CASE?

What Is Case? 145

The Possessive Case 145

The Nominative Case 148

The Objective Case 151

EXERCISE ANSWERS

Part 1—Nouns And Pronouns 159

Part 2—Verbs 169

Part 3—Other Parts Of Speech 179

Part 4—The Sentence 193

Part 5—Jobs Nouns And Pronouns Do In Sentences 199

Part 6—What Is Case? 207

PART 1
NOUNS AND PRONOUNS

GRAMMAR?

EXERCISE 1

Below are some of the benefits people get from understanding grammar. For the ones you are interested in having, rank them. If you'd prefer to create your own list, there are extra lines you can use at the bottom.

- ☐ can read faster with better understanding
- ☐ can find words that are misunderstood faster
- ☐ can look up words in a dictionary faster and easier.
- ☐ can explain ideas better
- ☐ can understand what people are saying better
- ☐ can write about ideas better

Any other benefits that are important to you:

- ☐ _____
- ☐ _____
- ☐ _____

SENTENCES & PARTS OF SPEECH

EXERCISE 2

What is a sentence?

_____

_____

EXERCISE 3

Make up two complete sentences and write them below. Underline the subject and verb of each sentence.

_____

_____

_____

_____

NOUNS

EXERCISE 4

What is a noun?

EXERCISE 5

What is a common noun?

NOUNS

EXERCISE 6

Make up a sentence with two or more common nouns. Write it down.

EXERCISE 7

What is a proper noun?

NOUNS

EXERCISE 8

Make up a sentence with two or more proper nouns. Write it down.

_____

_____

_____

_____

EXERCISE 9

Underline the common nouns in the sentences below and draw two lines under the proper nouns.

a) Some boys want to be firefighters when they grow up.

b) Lucas did, and he knew he would have to be very strong to pass the physical test required to become a firefighter.

c) He trained hard and knew he would be ready for the test when he was twenty-one.

d) He wasn't as certain that he could rush into a burning building to bring a person to safety.

e) Ten years later, he was a firefighter in Salem, Oregon and found all the courage he needed to go into a burning house and rescue two people.

NOUNS

EXERCISE 10

Write five or more sentences using common and proper nouns. Underline the common nouns once and the proper nouns twice.

Example:

Hannah had the courage to work as a nurse in Haiti after the earthquake.

PRONOUNS

EXERCISE 11

What is a pronoun?

_____

_____

_____

_____

EXERCISE 12

How can you use pronouns in your writing?

_____

_____

_____

_____

PRONOUNS

EXERCISE 13

Explain what a personal pronoun is and write down a made-up sentence using one.

EXERCISE 14

Explain what a possessive pronoun is and write down a made-up sentence using one.

PRONOUNS

EXERCISE 15

Rewrite each sentence by replacing each group of underlined words with a personal or possessive pronoun.

a) <u>Mary and I</u> were amazed to see how well Sadie, the new girl, played tennis.

b) <u>This girl</u> had been playing tennis since <u>this girl</u> was five years old, and <u>this girl</u> had had excellent coaches.

PRONOUNS

c) <u>These coaches</u> had taught <u>this girl</u> how to play tennis like a professional.

d) First prize in every tournament had been <u>belonged to this girl</u> since <u>this girl</u> had been twelve years old.

e) One day <u>this girl</u> lost her special, purple tennis racket. Her parents found one and asked her if it was <u>the racket that belonged to her.</u>

PRONOUNS

EXERCISE 16

Add to the sentences below by following the instruction on each line.

a) She congratulated _____. *(add a personal pronoun)*

b) That car is _____. *(add a possessive pronoun)*

c) They gave _____ *(add a personal pronoun)* many _____. *(add a noun)*

d) The teacher told _____ *(add a personal pronoun)* to rewrite the paper because _____ *(add a possessive pronoun)* was poorly written the first time.

EXERCISE 17

In the following story, write an appropriate personal or possessive pronoun in the blanks.

a) Let _____ tell _____ about our school trip to Europe.

b) After flying all night to London, _____ had to find our own luggage and carry _____ through the airport. My sister wasn't sure which suitcase was _____.

c) _____ were very tired, but our tour guide insisted that _____ walk around London all day to stay awake.

13

PRONOUNS

d) Finally after dinner, _____ returned to our hotel.

e) Our luggage had been all mixed up so _____ spent an hour sorting _____ out.

f) Our guide would hold up a suitcase and ask, "Whose is this?" The owner would say, "That is _____."

g) Then _____ would take _____ and go to _____ room to sleep.

h) The next day _____ were well rested and enjoyed seeing some beautiful parts of England.

EXERCISE 18

Explain what a reflexive pronoun is.

_____

_____

_____

_____

PRONOUNS

EXERCISE 19

Make up and write down three sentences using reflexive pronouns. Draw an arrow from the reflexive pronoun to the person or thing it refers to.

PRONOUNS

EXERCISE 20

In the following sentences, write a reflexive pronoun that makes sense in the blanks.

a) In the dining room, she poured _____ a drink to go with her meal.

b) The deer healed _____ by licking its wound.

c) The students fixed _____ a snack before studying at night.

d) Every year, we treated _____ to a French dinner on our birthday.

e) I _____ locked every door last night.

EXERCISE 21

Explain what a demonstrative pronoun is.

_____

_____

_____

_____

PRONOUNS

EXERCISE 22

Make up and write down three sentences using demonstrative pronouns.

PRONOUNS

EXERCISE 23

Rewrite each sentence by replacing the group of underlined words with a demonstrative pronoun.

a) I never thought he would do the thing they had been talking about.

b) The room being referred to is Mary's room.

c) Who owns the two computers indicated?

d) The first computer indicated belongs to Mary and the second computer indicated belongs to Martin.

PRONOUNS

EXERCISE 24

Explain what an interrogative pronoun is.

EXERCISE 25

Make up and write three questions using different interrogative pronouns.

PRONOUNS

EXERCISE 26

Underline the interrogative pronouns in these questions. (Not every question has an interrogative pronoun.)

a) <u>Who</u> is your favorite coach?

b) <u>Which</u> computer should I buy?

c) Why don't you come to the movies with us?

d) To <u>whom</u> should I send this letter?

e) <u>What</u> did you say to her?

f) How did you do that?

g) <u>Which</u> countries have you visited?

h) <u>Who</u> is the new photography instructor?

PRONOUNS

EXERCISE 27

Read the following story. In each blank write a personal, possessive or reflexive, demonstrative or interrogative pronoun that makes sense.

_____ is a story about my dog, Jemma. One day _____ were walking in a field when _____ spotted something and ran off across the field. _____ ran after _____ but had soon exhausted _____.

"_____ am I going to do? _____ should _____ go to?" _____ thought.

_____ started by going to a farmhouse on the far side of the field.

A woman opened the door and Jemma was standing next to _____.

Jemma furiously wagged her tail when _____ saw _____ and the woman asked, "Is _____ your dog?"

"Yes, _____ is _____," I said.

The woman told _____ that Jemma found her new puppy that had been lost in the field and brought _____ to _____.

_____ was so grateful that _____ gave Jemma a steak to eat!

21

PRONOUNS

EXERCISE 28

Explain what a relative pronoun is.

EXERCISE 29

Make up and write five sentences using different relative pronouns.

PRONOUNS

EXERCISE 30

Find and underline the relative pronoun in each sentence. Every sentence has one.

a) I learned about biology in the course <u>that</u> I just finished.

b) The teacher <u>who</u> taught me writing knew more about using language than anyone else I know.

c) You can borrow my dictionary, <u>which</u> is on the bookshelf above my desk.

d) Don't ask for <u>whom</u> I am making this dress; it is a secret.

e) The children <u>who</u> discovered the cave made it their secret meeting place.

f) The apprenticeship was <u>what</u> I needed to gain better organizational skills.

g) The coach <u>who</u> taught our team how to work together led us to the championship.

h) My last year in school, <u>which</u> was the most challenging, was the best preparation for my career.

i) Anna is the student <u>who</u> is managing this project.

j) That teacher taught me math in a way <u>that</u> helped me really understand it.

PRONOUNS

EXERCISE 31

Look for and underline the relative pronouns you find in these sentences. Not every sentence has one.

a) Alexander Graham Bell is the man for <u>whom</u> many telephone companies were named.

b) The Tulip Festival, <u>which</u> takes place in April, has flowers of all colors of the rainbow.

c) Brioche is a slightly sweet, egg bread <u>that</u> I could eat all day.

d) That computer is broken, but it will be fixed by tomorrow.

e) This protein shake is exactly what I need before exercising.

f) To prepare the dinner, the chef cooked the main dish and vegetables first and the dessert last.

g) Annie is the girl <u>who</u> oversees the project, so talk to her about helping with it.

h) There is an expensive jacket in lost and found. To whom does it belong?

i) The art project <u>that</u> won a national award will be displayed at the art show tomorrow.

j) Who is going on the field trip next week?

k) Everyone on the committee promised to do one job, but now they have forgotten what they promised to do.

l) What should we do about it?

PRONOUNS

EXERCISE 32

Complete the following sentences by adding a relative pronoun. You may add other words to the sentence if needed.

a) The high school students put on a play _____ was performed in May.

b) He was the student _____ earned a place on the Dean's List.

c) My friend for _____ I bought this gift turns sixteen tomorrow.

d) The school supplies _____ we bought in September are gone now.

e) The sweet, warm cocoa was precisely _____ they wanted on a cold, snowy day.

f) We handed our boarding passes to the flight attendant _____ invited us to board the plane.

g) She did well on the test because it was exactly _____ she had expected.

h) Our yearbook, _____ went on sale today, had a beautiful cover this year.

i) My teachers are people for _____ I will always be grateful.

j) Jupiter, _____ is the largest planet of our solar system, helps protect Earth from asteroids.

PRONOUNS

EXERCISE 33

Explain what an indefinite pronoun is.

EXERCISE 34

Write five sentences using a different indefinite pronoun in each.

PRONOUNS

EXERCISE 35

Find and underline the indefinite pronouns in each sentence. Every sentence has one.

a) <u>Everyone</u> on the track team will be competing in the meet next month.

b) The coach really hopes that <u>nobody</u> is ill that day.

c) <u>Several</u> of the boys on the relay team have world-class speed.

d) <u>No one</u> on the girls' team has that top speed but come very close.

e) As a unit, the girls' relay team can beat the <u>others</u> in the meet.

f) The hurdles challenge <u>everybody</u> who competes in that race.

g) <u>All</u> of the athletes' parents will cheer for them during the competition.

h) <u>Somebody</u> dressed as the school mascot cheered with the crowd.

PRONOUNS

EXERCISE 36

Find and underline the indefinite pronouns in each sentence. Not every sentence has one.

a) My mother baked enough cupcakes for <u>everyone</u> at the party to have two.

b) <u>Several</u> of the boys wanted to eat many more than two.

c) <u>A few</u> girls didn't want their cupcakes, so they gave them to the boys.

d) The party started in the beach house, but <u>somebody</u> asked if they could go swimming.

e) Then the party quickly became a beach party that <u>everybody</u> enjoyed in different ways.

f) <u>A few</u> of the boys were swimming and diving in the waves.

g) <u>Some</u> of the girls sat on blankets and soaked up the sun.

h) <u>Several</u> people walked along the beach picking up seashells.

i) It was so much fun that <u>many</u> of my guests stayed all day.

PRONOUNS

EXERCISE 37

Write an indefinite pronoun that makes sense in each sentence.

a) As guests arrived at her birthday party, Emily asked if they would like _____ to eat or drink.

b) Emily knew _____ had baked her a birthday cake, but she didn't know who.

c) _____ who brought a gift received a special thank you.

d) Emily made sure that _____ left the party hungry.

e) At the end of her party, Emily thanked _____ for coming.

PRONOUNS

EXERCISE 38

Write a paragraph or two using at least two relative pronouns and four indefinite pronouns. Underline these pronouns. Put an "r" above the relative pronouns and an "i" above the indefinite pronouns.

FINAL EXERCISE
39

Read the incomplete story below. Then complete the following sentences by writing common nouns or proper nouns that make sense in the blanks. Label each noun as common or proper.

a) Last _____, my family and I went on _____.

b) We rented a _____ at the beach in the state of _____.

c) We swam in the _____ and played beach volleyball for _____.

d) My sister, _____, and I both loved riding _____ on the beach.

e) It was the best _____ ever

FINAL EXERCISE

FINAL EXERCISE 40

Read the incomplete story below. Fill in the blanks with the pronouns that make the most sense.

a) This August _____ backpacked through the mountains of the western United States on a section of the Pacific Crest Trail.

b) _____ is _____ of the most beautiful hiking trails in America _____ extends from Canada to Mexico.

c) _____ had to carry _____ of the supplies _____ needed in our backpacks while walking from southern Washington State to northern California.

d) There were stations along the trail where _____ could resupply.

e) At each station, _____ had to ask _____, "_____ will _____ need for the next 200 miles?"

f) Along the trail, _____ made friends _____ came from all over the world.

g) _____ of the best places was Edison Lake, high in the Sierra Nevada Mountains of California.

h) _____ was an extraordinarily beautiful spot with a supply cabin at one end of the lake.

i) _____ hope to return to _____ every year.

PART 2
VERBS

VERBS

EXERCISE 1

What is a verb?

EXERCISE 2

Write a sentence about something you enjoy doing. Underline each verb.

VERBS

EXERCISE 3

What is an action verb?

EXERCISE 4

Write a sentence about doing your favorite sport or activity. Underline each action verb.

VERBS

EXERCISE 5

What is a being verb?

EXERCISE 6

Write a few sentences explaining how your favorite food looks, smells and tastes. Underline each being verb.

VERBS

EXERCISE 7

Underline all the verbs in the following sentences and draw an arrow from the verb to its subject. Mark B over each being verb and A over each action verb.

Examples:

          B
My parents <u>are</u> on vacation.

          A
They <u>will be gone</u> for one week.

a) Soccer is my favorite sport.

b) I played extensively for soccer teams last year.

c) My last coach said that I had become an excellent player.

d) All summer I exercised to stay in top physical condition.

e) In September, I seemed much stronger so I tried out for the varsity team.

f) I hope that I make it!

VERBS

EXERCISE 8

Write about an activity that you would like to do in the future. Include some sentences with two or more verbs working together. Underline each verb in every sentence.

VERBS

EXERCISE 9

Underline all verbs working together in the sentences below. Only underline the verbs, even when there is another part of speech interrupting them. For the sentences with two or more verbs for the same subject, underline each verb and draw an arrow to its subject.

Example:

My parents <u>are going</u> on vacation and <u>will be gone</u> for one week.

a) Will you finish your work soon?

b) We should be dressing and leaving for the concert in one hour.

c) We will drive into the city and eat in a wonderful restaurant first.

d) Then we will enjoy the spring performance of the symphony orchestra.

e) I do not know all of the music on the program for the evening but will enjoy it.

f) After the concert, we might use our backstage passes and meet all the musicians.

g) Then we will stay in a hotel for the night and drive home in the afternoon.

TRANSITIVE AND INTRANSITIVE VERBS

EXERCISE 10

What is a transitive verb?

_____
_____

EXERCISE 11

Make up three sentences using the following transitive verbs.

take _____
_____
_____

own _____
_____
_____

believe _____
_____
_____

TRANSITIVE AND INTRANSITIVE VERBS

EXERCISE 12

What is an intransitive verb?

_____

_____

EXERCISE 13

Make up three sentences using the following intransitive verbs.

catch _____

_____

_____

ride _____

_____

_____

laugh _____

_____

_____

TRANSITIVE AND INTRANSITIVE VERBS

EXERCISE 14

Some of these sentences contain transitive or intransitive verbs. Some have both. Underline the transitive verbs once and circle the direct objects. Underline the intransitive verbs twice.

a) Next month, I can take the test for a driving permit.

b) I have planned my driving lessons, so they are gradually more difficult.

c) I will drive my mother's car mostly and practice with her.

d) On my first lesson, I backed into a ditch at the roadside.

e) That was embarrassing!

f) After that, I backed up more slowly.

g) As I mastered each driving skill, I became a good driver.

h) After six months, I could take my final driving test and I passed it.

TRANSITIVE AND INTRANSITIVE VERBS

EXERCISE 15

Look up the verb *run* in a dictionary and find the definitions that fit for both sentences below. Use a dictionary that labels verbs as transitive or with object and intransitive or without object.

He will run the race tomorrow.

Write the correct definition of run for this sentence. Is run transitive or intransitive here?

_____

_____

_____

Please run upstairs and get your coat.

Write the correct definition of run for this sentence. Is run transitive or intransitive here?

_____

_____

_____

TRANSITIVE AND INTRANSITIVE VERBS

Many action verbs can be transitive or intransitive. Following the example, write a made up sentence for each action verb using it transitively and another sentence using it intransitively. Circle the direct object in each transitive verb sentence.

EXAMPLE:

sing

Transitive sentence   Tim *sings* his favorite (song) during every show.

Intransitive sentence   When he was in college, he *sang* at parties to earn spending money.

a) Action verb #1 *drink*

Transitive sentence _____

Intransitive sentence _____

TRANSITIVE AND INTRANSITIVE VERBS

b) Action verb #2 *write*

Transitive sentence _____

_____

_____

_____

Intransitive sentence _____

_____

_____

_____

c) Action verb #3 *celebrate*

Transitive sentence _____

_____

_____

_____

Intransitive sentence _____

_____

_____

_____

TRANSITIVE AND INTRANSITIVE VERBS

EXERCISE 17

All being verbs are intransitive. Write three original sentences using a form of *seem* or *become* as the intransitive verb.

EXERCISE 18

Write five original sentences using being verbs such as *looks*, *feels*, *smells*, *tastes*, etc., as the intransitive verb.

SUBJECT-VERB AGREEMENT

EXERCISE 19

In the following sentences, underline the verb in parentheses that agrees with the subject.

a) Jack (work, **works**) out the solution to the problem.

b) Can you (**bring**, brings) a cake to the picnic?

c) Jessica and Jill (learns, **learn**) many new things each year.

d) The volleyball team (**plays**, play) the champions next week.

e) Nobody (write, **writes**) music as well as you do.

f) Several of my friends (**ski**, skis) in Colorado every winter.

g) None of our teammates (**score**, scores) more goals than you.

h) Each of them (**gets**, get) a new backpack.

i) Someone (**is**, are) driving to the city tomorrow.

j) Both of the cakes (tastes, **taste**) great.

k) All of my schoolwork (take, **takes**) time to do.

l) Everyone in all the states (vote, **votes**) in November.

m) Some of the others (**leave**, leaves) for Asia in the morning.

n) Any of those sports (**seems**, seem) like fun.

o) Most of the berry pie (have, **has**) been eaten.

p) Neither of us (**qualifies**, qualify) for the final swim race.

SUBJECT-VERB AGREEMENT

EXERCISE 20

Read each sentence. If the verb of the sentence agrees with the subject, write OK on the line following the sentence. If the verb does not agree with the subject of the sentence, write the correct form of the verb on the line following the sentence.

a) Robert or Ethan are riding with me. _____

b) Each of the games take two hours to play. _____

c) Grasses and a certain type of moss covers the forest floor. _____

d) All of my songs is saved in my tablet. _____

e) Everyone with passports are in this line. _____

f) A computer, pencil, and eraser is required for that class. _____

g) Either of those paths are the correct one to take. _____

h) Some of my brothers are here. _____

i) Several of the stars in the Milky Way Galaxy are red giants. _____

j) Everybody in the gym were surprised at the game's score. _____

k) Most of my work require specialized knowledge. _____

l) Anabelle or her friends plans to decorate the hall. _____

THE FOUR FORMS OF VERBS

EXERCISE 21

Show the four forms for the verbs listed below. Note: If you don't know a form of a verb, you can look it up. A good online dictionary for this purpose is www.oxforddictionaries.com.

a) Show the four forms for the regular verb *talk*.

Infinitive: _____

Present participle: _____

Past: _____

Past participle: _____

b) Show the four forms for the irregular verb *choose*.

Infinitive: _____

Present participle: _____

Past: _____

Past participle: _____

THE FOUR FORMS OF VERBS

EXERCISE 22

Write some sentences about your interests using the different verb forms indicated in parentheses. You may use a dictionary to learn a verb form you don't know.

EXAMPLE:

begin   Today I am going to *begin* guitar lessons. (infinitive)

or

Today I *am beginning* guitar lessons for the third time. (present participle)

Last year I *began* guitar lessons for the second time then stopped practicing. (past)

Often I *have begun* guitar lessons, but I *haven't continued* long enough to master the guitar. (past participle)

a) *come*

(present participle) Today _____

_____

(past) Yesterday _____

_____

(past participle) Often in the past _____

_____

THE FOUR FORMS OF VERBS

b) *do*

(infinitive) Today _____

_____

(present participle) Today _____

_____

(past) Yesterday _____

_____

(past participle) Often _____

_____

c) *give*

(present participle) Today _____

_____

(past) Yesterday _____

_____

(past participle) For several years _____

_____

THE FOUR FORMS OF VERBS

d) *know* or *throw*

(infinitive) Today _____

_____

(present participle) Today _____

_____

(past) Yesterday _____

_____

(past participle) Often _____

_____

VERB TENSES

EXERCISE 23

Complete the sentences in the present tense using one of the following verbs:

cause(s)   eat(s)   wake(s)   care(s)   speak(s)   walk(s)   take(s)

a) Sean _____ French fluently.

b) Our neighbors _____ to the park every day.

c) The phases of our moon _____ the tides.

d) Elise _____ her final exam today.

e) We always _____ lunch at noon.

f) Nurses _____ for sick people.

g) He _____ up at 7:00 every morning.

VERB TENSES

EXERCISE 24

Write a paragraph in the present tense explaining how to do something in a sport or activity you like. Some examples are how to serve in volleyball or tennis, how to do a penalty kick in soccer, how to play a musical scale, how to saddle a horse, how to use a pottery wheel, and so on.

VERB TENSES

EXERCISE 25

Complete each sentence in the past tense using the correct form of the verb and any additional words given. Note: If you don't know the past form of a verb, you can look it up. A good online dictionary for this purpose is www.oxforddictionaries.com.

a) We _____ to see a great play last week. (go)

b) The play _____ a very good comedy. (be)

c) _____ you _____ it too? (do/see)

d) Yes, we _____ it two days ago. (see)

e) The actors _____ their comedic roles very well. (perform)

f) After the play, we _____ dinner at a new restaurant. (eat)

g) _____ that too late to eat dinner? (be/not)

h) Not at all, we _____ over a light meal and _____ the play. (relax/discuss)

i) We _____ to get home too early. (do/not/like)

VERB TENSES

EXERCISE 26

Write a paragraph in the past tense about something you finished or accomplished last year. Explain what you did and what you liked about it.

VERB TENSES

EXERCISE 27

Complete each sentence in the future tense using *will/'ll*, *will not/won't*, *Shall I?* or *Shall we?* + verb that makes sense.

a) Her friends asked her, "Where _____ we _____ lunch?

b) Wait for me. It _____ me long to get ready.

c) I _____ ready for the dance in ten minutes.

d) She asked her mother, _____ I _____ the vase of flowers on the dining room table?

e) He loves that restaurant and _____ anywhere else.

f) Let's go to the movies. What _____ we _____?

g) Do you think you _____ that team next spring?

h) Our soccer team _____ probably _____ that opponent in the championship game next week.

i) Next November, I _____ probably _____ a short novel.

j) I'm going to that party tomorrow. Do you think you _____ _____?

k) Janice is worried that she _____ her paintings in time for the art show.

l) I'm sure Kyle _____ his promise.

VERB TENSES

EXERCISE 28

Write a paragraph in the future tense about something you plan to do next year. Explain what you will do and what interests you about it.

VERB TENSES

EXERCISE 29

Label each noun, pronoun, and verb in the following sentences.

EXAMPLE:

                                  n.   v.   pron.   pron.   v.
The black dog came to her when she called.

a) She will study biology in college.

b) My family takes a vacation in Hawaii every year.

c) John wrote a short novel last summer.

d) Joyce bought a new dress for the dance.

e) Are you going to the volleyball game?

FINAL EXERCISE 30

Some of these sentences have correct verb forms and some do not. Correct incorrect verb forms in the blanks. If a sentence has the correct verb form, write "OK" in the blank. You may refer to Understanding Sentences or a dictionary if needed.

a) Last week, we swim at the beach. _____

b) Last night, temperatures go below freezing so the fountain freezes. _____

c) It costed ten dollars to go to the school dance last weekend. _____

d) They has a meeting today. _____

e) He began playing soccer ten years ago. _____

f) In the past, we have drunk well water, but now we drank bottled water. _____

g) Sara takes her final exam last week. _____

h) My mother has knowed her best friend for forty-five years. _____

i) Last month, Jill feels so happy when she travelled to meet her friends from high school. _____

j) Jason ran a four-minute mile yesterday. _____

k) I brang a pie to my family's holiday feast. _____

l) Shelly written a letter to her U.S. Senator about an unfair law and it be changed. _____

FINAL EXERCISE

FINAL EXERCISE 31

Complete each sentence by making the verb given agree with the subject and the tense given. Do not use any references.

a) Everyone _____ (go, present) to the volleyball game today.

b) Next month, Jennifer and Sierra _____ (be, future) on their way to Europe.

c) When I was 4 years old, I _____ (begin, past) taking dance lessons.

d) Every year, each of the students _____ (take, present) on difficult community projects.

e) This year, both my sisters _____ (study, present) at the colleges of their choice.

f) James _____ (drink, past) water with minerals before every soccer game.

g) All the students _____ (sing, past) well in the choir performance.

h) Because they had practiced so hard, they _____ (know, past) they would do well in the competition.

i) I _____ (bring, past) snacks to the Student Council meeting.

j) We _____ (write, past) over ten essays in the past few months.

PART 3
OTHER PARTS OF SPEECH

ADJECTIVES

EXERCISE 1

What is an adjective?

_____

_____

_____

EXERCISE 2

Make up a sentence using two or more adjectives.

_____

_____

_____

EXERCISE 3

Explain why each type of article is an adjective.

a or *an*: _____

the: _____

ADJECTIVES

EXERCISE 4

Make up a sentence using *a*.

_____

_____

EXERCISE 5

Make up a sentence using *an*.

_____

_____

EXERCISE 6

Make up a sentence using *the*.

_____

_____

ADJECTIVES

Underline each adjective in the following sentences. Label descriptive adjectives with adj. and label articles with art.

EXAMPLE:

       art. adj.   adj.   adj.
The black cat climbs over that fence every day.

a) The day in early May was sunny and breezy.

b) We enjoyed a delicious dinner at the French restaurant.

c) I suggest you buy that small computer you found in the local newspaper.

d) That Arabian horse climbs those mountain trails easily.

e) Which of the chocolate cupcakes are gluten-free?

ADJECTIVES

EXERCISE 8

Find 20 different adjectives in a dictionary and make a list of them. Write some paragraphs using all those adjectives. It can be fun or funny.

1. _____ 2. _____ 3. _____
4. _____ 5. _____ 6. _____
7. _____ 8. _____ 9. _____
10. _____ 11. _____ 12. _____
13. _____ 14. _____ 15. _____
16. _____ 17. _____ 18. _____
19. _____ 20. _____

ADJECTIVES

EXERCISE 9

Label each noun, pronoun, verb, adjective, and article in the following sentences.

EXAMPLE:

    art.   adj.   adj.   n.   v.   pron.
    The huge, black dog ran to her.

a) A lemon cake makes a perfect dessert.

b) She found that reference in the school library.

c) Those fir trees behind the building are ancient.

d) I am studying two languages this year.

e) Can you meet me in the old, science lab?

ADVERBS

EXERCISE 10

a) What is an adverb?

_____

_____

_____

b) Make up three sentences using adverbs to modify these parts of speech:

a verb _____

_____

_____

an adjective _____

_____

_____

another adverb _____

_____

_____

ADVERBS

> **EXERCISE 11**

Underline each adverb in the following sentences. Draw an arrow to the word the adverb is modifying. Every sentence has at least one adverb. Some sentences have more than one.

ADVERBS MODIFYING VERBS:

a) Zack sprinted easily across the field.

b) The raccoon climbed the tree carefully.

c) He will soon be sixteen years old.

d) She runs better in the morning and really hates evening competitions.

ADVERBS MODIFYING ADJECTIVES:

e) Your dress is a beautiful red color.

f) These are extraordinarily delicious cookies.

g) That dark red horse is much taller than she is.

h) The deep blue sky against the brilliant white clouds accentuated all the colors of the landscape.

ADVERBS

ADVERBS MODIFYING OTHER ADVERBS:

i) Zack reads very accurately.

j) My new computer runs much faster than I expected.

k) I have never seen such an amazingly deep blue sky.

WHAT DO THE ADVERBS MODIFY IN THESE SENTENCES?

l) John writes French very quickly and reads it even faster.

m) I really appreciate your completely honest answer.

n) We drove past many, bright green fields in Oregon this spring.

ADVERBS

EXERCISE 12

These sentences have poorly placed modifiers. Rewrite them to change where the modifier is placed so the meaning is clear.

a) Mary walked up slowly the road.

b) Jack will be turning soon eighteen years old.

c) Put away quickly your books.

d) The house gray became in the summer hot.

e) I gave her gladly new clothes for work.

ADVERBS

> **EXERCISE 13**

Label each noun, pronoun, verb, adjective, and adverb in the following sentences. You don't have to label the articles.

> EXAMPLE:
>
>   *adv.*   *adj.* *adj.* *n.*   *adv.* *v.*   *pron.*
> The extremely huge, black dog quickly ran to her.

a) They always sailed across the deep blue Pacific every summer.

b) Happily, the whole family snowboarded well during that visit to Mt. Hood.

c) Did you really write an adventure novel?

d) I attended an incredibly useful soccer camp last fall.

e) Anna serves a volleyball blazingly fast.

f) He runs faster than everyone else on the track team.

g) French food tastes so good.

h) The chef tasted the sauce twice.

COMPARISON

EXERCISE 14

The choices are given in parentheses. Underline the correct one.

> EXAMPLE: She is the (<u>prettier</u>, prettiest) of the two cousins.

a) Which do you like (more, most), coffee or tea?

b) The weather is (more better, best, better) than yesterday.

c) He is the (less, least) talkative of the three friends.

d) That book was the (easier, most easy, easiest) of all the books on that level.

e) The beach camping trip was (most wonderful, wonderfuler, more wonderful) than our other summer trip to the mountains.

f) John is the (taller, most tall, tallest) of the three brothers.

g) My puppy is (more, most, much) intelligent than her sister.

h) She always likes to play music (more loudly, louder, the loudest) than her roommate.

COMPARISON

EXERCISE 15

Here or on your computer, write several paragraphs comparing two or more interesting things that you already know about. You could compare two or more sports or sports teams, types of art or music, hobbies, and so on.

MODIFIERS MADE FROM VERBS

EXERCISE 16

Explain what a participle is.

_____

_____

_____

_____

EXERCISE 17

Make up a sentence using a participle for *work*:

as an adjective: _____

_____

_____

to form a verb tense with two or more verbs: _____

_____

_____

MODIFIERS MADE FROM VERBS

EXERCISE 18

Underline the modifying participles in the following sentences. In the blank, write the word being modified.

EXAMPLE: The <u>laughing</u> child jumped into the pool.   child

a) The swimming horse crossed the river easily. _____

b) Improved by a new design, the house was remodeled in the summer. _____

c) Jane left the car running while she ran into the house to get something. _____

d) They were eager to hear the visiting professor's lecture. _____

e) The exhilarated runner was the first to finish the race. _____

f) The autumn leaves floated in the swirling wind. _____

g) His written work is excellent. _____

h) The teacher helped his students with a specially planned algebra lesson. _____

i) In the fall, fish can hide under the leaves floating along the edge of the river. _____

MODIFIERS MADE FROM VERBS

EXERCISE 19

Complete each sentence using one of the verbs given as a participle that modifies.

EXAMPLE:

give Beth had a *giving* family that supported their community.

vote   sing   cry   stop   study   tire   ride   spin   haunt   excite   evolve

a) The _____ house frightened some people.

b) The new mother calmed her _____ baby.

c) Samantha needed new _____ clothes before her horseback riding competition.

d) The students were very _____ because they had studied late the night before.

e) Women don't have _____ rights everywhere in the world.

f) Michael controlled the _____ ball and passed it to his teammate.

g) Both biology and chemistry are _____ sciences.

h) The seniors planned an _____ party for all the students.

i) The _____ cars created a traffic jam.

j) The choir gave an inspired _____ performance.

MODIFIERS MADE FROM VERBS

EXERCISE 20

Write complete sentences using the participial phrases given.

Example: *swimming in the ocean currents*

Swimming in the ocean currents, the dolphins leapt and glided past our boat.

a) *singing as loud as possible*

b) *finding the solution to the problem*

c) *dancing and laughing the night away*

MODIFIERS MADE FROM VERBS

d) *guaranteed to be fresh*

e) *thrilled to hear the good news*

f) *written originally in French*

MODIFIERS MADE FROM VERBS

EXERCISE 21

Rewrite these sentences so the participial phrases are placed where they make the meaning clear. You may need to add or change some words.

EXAMPLE: Checking the weather, sunny skies were forecast for the next two days. (Are the skies checking the weather?)

Rewrite: Checking the weather, she saw that sunny skies were forecast for the next two days.

a) Gazing into the mirror, her dress looked perfect for the dance.

b) Repaired and polished, I picked up my watch from the jeweler.

MODIFIERS MADE FROM VERBS

c) Invigorated from the hike, food and water were welcome when we returned home.

d) Flying across the finish line, the referee signaled that the cyclist won the race.

e) After grazing the organic grass field, the farmer moved his cows into the barn.

PREPOSITIONS

EXERCISE 22

What is a preposition?

EXERCISE 23

Make up two sentences using prepositions.

PREPOSITIONS

EXERCISE 24

Underline the prepositions in these sentences. Not every sentence has one.

a) Jamie walked <u>into</u> the field where his horse, Tolly, was grazing.

b) Tolly ran <u>to</u> Jamie when he saw him.

c) Then Jamie quickly saddled Tolly.

d) They started riding <u>along</u> the edge <u>of</u> the forest.

e) Suddenly, Jamie saw a small person scurry <u>behind</u> a fallen tree.

f) Tolly sprinted <u>toward</u> the person and jumped <u>over</u> the fallen tree.

g) Jamie turned fast and saw a forest gnome, who promptly disappeared!

EXERCISE 25

Write a sentence with a preposition in it. Explain what this sentence means. Then change the preposition and explain what the sentence means now. Do this a third time. Have fun with it!

a) Your sentence using a preposition:

_____

_____

85

PREPOSITIONS

Explain the meaning:

b) The same sentence using a different preposition:

Explain its meaning now:

c) The same sentence using another preposition:

Explain its meaning now:

PREPOSITIONS

EXERCISE 26

Underline each prepositional phrase in these sentences. Every sentence has one. Some sentences have more than one. If you aren't sure that a word is acting as a preposition, you can use a dictionary to look it up.

> Hint: *To* followed by a verb is an infinitive.
> *To* followed by a noun or pronoun is a prepositional phrase.

a) In 2017, there was a total eclipse of the sun in Oregon.

b) My friends and I prepared ahead of time and bought special glasses.

c) These enabled us to look at the sun and protect our eyes from damage.

d) To get the best view, we sat high on a hill in a meadow.

e) As the moon's shadow fell across the sun, the bright summer morning grew darker and darker.

f) When the moon had completely blocked the sun, the day turned into a cool night and the wind started to blow.

g) Then the shadow moved past the sun and its rays gradually shone down on us again.

h) Now, I fully appreciate the warmth and light of our sun.

PREPOSITIONS

EXERCISE 27

Refer to these:

ADJECTIVE (adj.)

Modifies: nouns or pronouns

Answers:

1) Which?

2) What kind of?

3) How many?

ADVERB (adv.)

Modifies: verbs, adjectives, or adverbs

Answers:

1) When?

2) Where?

3) How?

4) To what degree, or how much?

Then, underline the prepositional phrases in the following sentences. Determine what word the prepositional phrase is modifying and draw an arrow to it. Above the prepositional phrase, note if the phrase is acting as an adjective (adj.) or an adverb (adv.).

PREPOSITIONS

EXAMPLE:

The flowers <u>in the garden</u> are blooming. *adj.*

a) The children's laughter during the break was delightful.

b) My grandmother always sat in her favorite chair.

c) Our campsite beside the river was absolutely beautiful.

d) Would you rather write with a pen or pencil?

e) This spring, we saw birds of many kinds.

f) My dog always gallops to my side to greet me when I come home.

g) My grandfather painted over one hundred watercolors.

h) Our group hiked through the forest to a waterfall.

PREPOSITIONS

EXERCISE 28

Without using any prepositional phrases, write a description of a bridge you have seen or crossed. Were you able to communicate the full picture that way?

Now using any prepositional phrases you want, revise your writing. Were you able to describe the bridge clearly?

PREPOSITIONS

EXERCISE 29

Label each noun, pronoun, verb, and preposition in the following sentences.

a) Our girls' volleyball team just won enough games for the district tournament in the fall of 2017.

b) Their first opponent was a team they had already beaten in September.

c) They easily won that match in two hours.

d) Next, they had to play a top-seeded school that they had never played before.

e) Before that match, the team practiced late into the night.

f) Their next game was filled with tension as the lead changed many times.

g) Finally, our team triumphed and advanced to the State Championship.

h) Everyone in our school was happy they had seen that.

CONJUNCTIONS

EXERCISE 30

What is a conjunction?

_____

_____

EXERCISE 31

Join these sentences with conjunctions.

a) I would like to go to the play with you. I don't have enough money.

_____

_____

b) Do you want to play softball this spring? Do you want to run track?

_____

_____

_____

CONJUNCTIONS

EXERCISE 32

Each sentence below has a coordinating conjunction (FANBOYS). Find it and underline it.

a) I would like to go to the concert, <u>but</u> I haven't earned enough money for the ticket.

b) I have to study <u>so</u> I won't be able to go to the movies tonight.

c) My mother does not ride horses <u>nor</u> does she ski, <u>but</u> all her daughters do. (*This sentence has two conjunctions.*)

d) Would you like chicken <u>or</u> fish for dinner?

e) The students learned to waltz <u>and</u> salsa before the school dance.

f) Rigo is small, <u>yet</u> he is one of our best players.

g) He spent his free time inventing new recipes, <u>for</u> he loved to delight people with new foods.

CONJUNCTIONS

EXERCISE 33

Each sentence has a correlative conjunction. Find it and underline it.

a) <u>Both</u> plums <u>and</u> peaches ripen in the summer.

b) The children <u>either</u> played tag <u>or</u> swam all day.

c) <u>Neither</u> Sam <u>nor</u> Ty like to play goalie.

d) He <u>not only</u> studied French <u>but also</u> Chinese and Japanese.

e) I didn't know <u>whether</u> she was joking <u>or not</u>.

f) This dessert is <u>not only</u> sugar-free <u>but</u> it is <u>also</u> organic.

g) This fall, you may choose <u>either</u> volleyball <u>or</u> soccer.

h) <u>Both</u> the children <u>and</u> their parents learned a lot at the county fair.

CONJUNCTIONS

EXERCISE 34

Each sentence has a subordinating conjunction. Find it and underline it twice. Notice the dependent clause the conjunction begins and underline the whole clause once.

a) Until I walked through that forest, I didn't understand its magic.

b) I first noticed the butterflies of all colors because there were hundreds of them.

c) I knew something was different when I saw a butterfly land on a flower and make it grow.

d) Before a butterfly touched a flower, it had a normal blossom.

e) After a butterfly landed on a flower, it grew four times the normal size with huge flowers.

f) As long as I stayed on the path, I could enjoy the magic.

g) Bad things happened whenever I left the path.

h) When I saw a flash of pure white and followed it off the path, the wind howled and it started to rain.

i) Although I was frightened by the storm, I continued to chase the white thing into a cave and was astonished to find a unicorn!

CONJUNCTIONS

EXERCISE 35

Write complete sentences using the words given plus a conjunction and any other words you need.

EXAMPLE: She, dances, sings

She *not only* dances *but also* sings quite well.

or

She dances *and* sings every weekend.

or

Because she dances *and* sings, she is perfect for the role.

a) eat, steak, potatoes

b) go, movies, work

c) like, fruits, vegetables

d) sunny day, swimming, beach

e) never, know, to shake hands, give hugs, meet

f) team won, we celebrated

g) snowing, will go skiing

INTERJECTIONS

EXERCISE 36

What is an interjection?

EXERCISE 37

Make up three sentences using interjections with correct punctuation.

THE EIGHT PARTS OF SPEECH

FINAL EXERCISE 38

Underline and label each prepositional phrase, dependent and independent clause in the following sentences. If needed, you may look up any word in a dictionary.

Prepositional phrase = prep. phr.
Dependent clause = dep. cl.
Independent clause = ind. cl.

EXAMPLE:

      dep. clause   ind. cl.   prep. phr.
<u>Whenever we awaken early,</u> we see the local deer grazing <u>in the fields</u>.

a) It was a beautiful summer day, and we were picking blackberries.

b) Buzzing bees were collecting nectar and pollen from the flowers.

c) Ouch! I mistakenly stepped on one of the honey bees, and it stung me.

d) Because my foot started to swell, I went inside and put ice on it.

e) When the ice made my foot feel better, I went back to the blackberry patch.

f) After I had picked a huge bowl of blackberries, I took them home.

g) I will either eat them raw or bake them in a pie. Yuuummmm!

FINAL EXERCISE 39

Label each part of speech in the following sentences. If needed, you may look up any word in a dictionary.

Noun=n.
Pronoun=pron.
Verb=v.
Adjective=adj. Label articles separately as art.
Adverb=adv.
Preposition=prep.
Conjunction=conj.
Interjection=intj.

EXAMPLE:

```
 conj.   pron.   v.    adv.  pron.  v.  art.  adj.    n.    v.   prep. art.   n.
Whenever  we  awaken  early,  we  see  the  local  deer  grazing  in  the  fields.
```

a) It was a beautiful summer day, and we were picking blackberries.

b) Buzzing bees were collecting nectar and pollen from the flowers.

c) Ouch! I mistakenly stepped on one of the honey bees, and it stung me.

d) Because my foot started to swell, I went inside and put ice on it.

e) When the ice made my foot feel better, I went back to the blackberry patch.

f) After I had picked a huge bowl of blackberries, I took them home.

g) I will either eat them raw or bake them in a pie. Yuuummmm!

PART 4
THE SENTENCE

THE SENTENCE

EXERCISE 1

What is a sentence?

_____
_____
_____
_____

EXERCISE 2

What is the subject of a sentence?

_____
_____
_____
_____

THE SENTENCE

EXERCISE 3

Write down two made-up sentences and underline the subjects.

_____

_____

_____

_____

_____

EXERCISE 4

Write down two more made-up sentences and underline the verb of the sentence plus any modifying words with it.

_____

_____

_____

_____

_____

THE SENTENCE

EXERCISE 5

What is a clause?

_____
_____

Your example of a clause:

_____
_____
_____

EXERCISE 6

What is an independent clause?

_____
_____

THE SENTENCE

EXERCISE 7

What is the difference between a dependent clause and an independent clause?

_____

_____

_____

_____

EXERCISE 8

Write two examples of an independent clause:

_____

_____

_____

_____

_____

THE SENTENCE

EXERCISE 9

Write two examples of a dependent clause:

THE SENTENCE

EXERCISE 10

Find and underline the subject(s) of each sentence. If the subject is understood, write it in.

a) Almost every weekend, <u>I</u> hike through the woods with my friends.

b) <u>Jill</u> and <u>Susan</u> are going with me this weekend.

c) <u>Jill</u> and <u>I</u> will be walking on the trails, but not Susan.

d) <u>Susan</u> will run cross-country most likely and meet us at the lake.

e) <u>She</u> walks with us for a little while, but <u>I</u> can see that <u>she</u> really wants to run.

f) <u>I</u> tell her right away.

g) (<u>you</u>) Go ahead and meet us later.

h) Where do <u>you</u> want to meet?

i) <u>We</u> should meet at the lake by noon and eat a picnic lunch there.

THE SENTENCE

EXERCISE 11

Find and underline the verb(s) of each sentence.

a) Almost every weekend, I <u>hike</u> through the woods with my friends.

b) Jill and Susan <u>are going</u> with me this weekend.

c) Jill and I <u>will be walking</u> on the trails, but not Susan.

d) Susan <u>will run</u> cross-country most likely and <u>meet</u> us at the lake.

e) She <u>walks</u> with us for a little while, but I <u>can see</u> that she really <u>wants</u> to <u>run</u>.

f) I <u>tell</u> her right away.

g) <u>Go</u> ahead and <u>meet</u> us later.

h) Where <u>do</u> you <u>want</u> to <u>meet</u>?

i) We <u>should meet</u> at the lake by noon and <u>eat</u> a picnic lunch there.

THE SENTENCE

EXERCISE 12

Write five sentences or more describing something you enjoyed doing last week. Find and underline the subject of each sentence. Then find and double underline the verb of each sentence.

SENTENCE ERRORS

EXERCISE 13

Some of these sentences are complete and some are sentence fragments. Label each fragment with *fragment* and each complete sentence with *complete*.

a) Since it is time to make my presentation and I've been ready for two weeks.

b) She laughed.

c) Because Garrett loves to snowboard.

d) I don't know who the speaker is going to be today.

e) Finish reading your book tonight.

f) When I have written my novel and had it published.

g) As beautifully as they could sing.

h) All around the campus.

SENTENCE ERRORS

EXERCISE 14

Some of these sentences are fine, and some are run-on sentences. Find the run-ons and label them.

a) He is reading a new book, it is about the American Revolution.

b) My favorite sport is volleyball because I like the teamwork.

c) Jeremy practices playing the guitar all the time, he plays for anyone who will listen and asks their opinion of the song.

d) On the track team, she sprinted and jumped hurdles and practiced relay races.

e) We sang together, my brother ate pizza, my mother ate a salad.

f) During the holidays, I like cooking with my family and learning how to make new dishes.

g) We just got a new puppy, he needs a lot of training, we don't know what to name him.

h) The weather was great the stadium had comfortable seats, our team was winning, it was a great day of watching the game.

SENTENCE ERRORS

EXERCISE 15

Take the sentence fragments you found in the exercise 13 and make them complete sentences.

a) _____

_____

_____

b) _____

_____

_____

c) _____

_____

_____

d) _____

_____

_____

e) _____

_____

_____

SENTENCE ERRORS

EXERCISE 16

Take the run-ons you found in exercise 14 and fix them with periods or conjunctions or both.

a)

b)

c)

d)

e)

THREE WAYS TO BUILD SENTENCES

EXERCISE 17

Underline and label each prepositional phrase, dependent clause and independent clause in the following sentences. If you would like to look in a dictionary to verify the part of speech of a word, you may do that.

Prepositional phrase = prep. phr.
Dependent clause = dep. cl.
Independent clause = ind. cl.

Hint: **To** followed by a verb is an infinitive.
To followed by a noun or pronoun is a prepositional phrase.

EXAMPLE:

      dep. clause   *ind. cl.*   *prep. phr.*
Whenever we awaken early, we see the local deer grazing in the fields.

a) As the days grow longer in the spring, everything seems full of life in the garden.

b) I'm planting flowers throughout the garden, but the boys are preparing the soil to plant vegetables in the back.

c) Since the mornings are still frosty in March, I can only plant flowers that can grow in the cold weather.

THREE WAYS TO BUILD SENTENCES

d) Most vegetables will have to wait until the weather warms up.

e) When it is April, we can plant all the flowers.

f) We should plant all the vegetables before May at the latest.

g) In June, the sun can be so hot that all the plants need more water.

h) The flowers are so pretty in May and June.

i) They make the garden look beautiful, and they attract honeybees, butterflies and hummingbirds.

j) By August, many of the vegetables and berries are so ripe that they are easy to pick and delicious to eat.

THREE WAYS TO BUILD SENTENCES

EXERCISE 18

Complete the sentences by adding a clause.

a) _____ around the campus most evenings.

b) During spring break, _____.

c) _____ who played well.

d) Because I wanted to study art, _____ _____.

e) _____, but eventually we found our way home.

f) She went to Florence, Italy _____.

g) _____ that I really liked.

h) Even though my favorite sport is volleyball, _____ _____.

THREE WAYS TO BUILD SENTENCES

EXERCISE 19

Complete the sentences by adding a clause and a phrase.

a) _____, I like riding my bike ____ _____.

b) Whenever it snows, _____.

c) In the fall, _____.

d) _____, I'll learn to drive a car ____ _____.

e) I plan to try out for the varsity team, but _____ _____.

FINAL EXERCISE

FINAL EXERCISE 20

In the following story, there are some sentence fragments and a run-on sentence. Find them and underline them. Then fix them on the lines below.

One of my favorite authors is E. B. White. He wrote the children's book, *Charlotte's Web,* about a clever spider and her special friend, Wilbur the pig. Such a beautiful book. Another children's book he wrote is *The Trumpet of the Swan*, which is about trumpeter swans.

He also wrote articles for *The New Yorker* magazine, some were funny, some were serious and pointed out areas where change was needed, all were well written. I enjoy his funny articles the most. Like an amusing one about a mother raccoon in his backyard.

a) _____

b) _____

c) _____

FINAL EXERCISE

FINAL EXERCISE 21

Write several paragraphs about a time you learned to do something that you really liked. It can be real or made-up, serious or funny. Include each of these:

a) A simple sentence

b) A compound sentence

c) A complex sentence

Label each one.

PART 5
JOBS NOUNS AND PRONOUNS DO IN SENTENCES

JOBS NOUNS AND PRONOUNS DO IN SENTENCES

EXERCISE 1

What is the complete subject of a sentence?

EXERCISE 2

Make up and write three sentences that have complete subjects, and underline those.

JOBS NOUNS AND PRONOUNS DO IN SENTENCES

EXERCISE 3

Take a paragraph you have already written or write a new paragraph. In each of your sentences, underline the complete subject and label the noun or pronoun that is the simple subject with an S. (If the subject of any sentence is an implied "you," write "subject=you" on the same line.)

JOBS NOUNS AND PRONOUNS DO IN SENTENCES

EXERCISE 4

In the sentences below, underline the complete subject and label the noun or pronoun that is the simple subject with an S. (If the subject of any sentence is an implied "you," write "subject=you" on the same line.)

a) Quinn and Kostya, looking for edible mushrooms, were walking in the woods yesterday.

b) When they reached the pond, they saw a mysterious boy fishing on the other side.

c) They had never seen the boy before and wondered who he was.

d) Quinn thought they should walk around the pond and say hello.

e) The adventurous Kostya convinced her to go climb the big pine tree instead.

f) They started to walk away toward the big pine.

g) Wait! Did they hear something?

h) It was the boy calling to them.

i) Quinn and Kostya turned to wait for the boy but he had disappeared.

j) They quickly ran to the last spot that they had seen him but he was gone.

DIRECT OBJECTS

EXERCISE 5

What is a direct object?

EXERCISE 6

Make up three sentences that have direct objects and underline those.

DIRECT OBJECTS

EXERCISE 7

Write a brief short story. It can be true or made up. Include sentences that have direct objects and underline each one in your story.

DIRECT OBJECTS

EXERCISE 8

In each of the sentences below, label every noun or pronoun that is a simple subject with an S. Where there is a complete subject, underline it. Also label every noun or pronoun that is a direct object with D.O.

Note: Not every sentence has a direct object.

a) Next week I will enter my artwork in a state art show.

b) First, I must create my pottery so it has time to dry fully.

c) Next I will paint several paintings.

d) Then I planned the design for some pen and ink drawings.

e) Once all the pieces of art are dry and ready, I will sign my name on each one.

f) The art show is tomorrow and my artwork is ready.

g) Later in the evening, my friends and I cleaned my art studio and made it ready for visitors.

INDIRECT OBJECTS

EXERCISE 9

What is an indirect object?

EXERCISE 10

Make up three sentences that have indirect objects and underline them.

INDIRECT OBJECTS

EXERCISE 11

Write a paragraph about something that interests you or a brief short story. Include sentences that have indirect objects. Once you have finished your writing, underline all the direct objects and circle all the indirect objects.

INDIRECT OBJECTS

> **EXERCISE 12**

In each of the sentences below, label every noun or pronoun that is a simple subject with an S. Where there is a complete subject, underline it. (If the subject is an implied "you," write "Subject=you" on the same line.)

Also label every noun or pronoun that is a direct object with D.O. and those that are indirect objects with I.O.

Note: Not every sentence has a direct and indirect object, and some sentences may have two.

a) On the morning of my birthday, my friends gave me a gift.

b) Then we celebrated with a special breakfast.

c) Later my brother gave my friends and me a ride to the beach so we could swim.

d) When we returned, my favorite aunt threw a surprise party for me.

e) My friends brought me cards and candy.

f) We played games and music all evening and had a great time!

THE OBJECT OF A PREPOSITION

EXERCISE 13

What is the object of a preposition?

EXERCISE 14

Make up three sentences that have prepositional phrases and underline the objects of the prepositions.

THE OBJECT OF A PREPOSITION

EXERCISE 15

Write a short paragraph that describes how to do something you like to do. It could be dribbling a soccer ball, cooking a particular dish, taking a photograph, reading a book, learning a new language, or anything you like to do. Once your paragraph is written, underline all the prepositional phrases and circle all the objects of those prepositions.

THE OBJECT OF A PREPOSITION

EXERCISE 16

Build each sentence by following the instructions on each line. Label the noun or pronoun that is the object of the preposition with O.P.

a) They ran _____.
   (add a prepositional phrase)

b) They ran _____.
   (add a prepositional phrase) to earn money
   _____.
   (add a prepositional phrase)

c) Early _____,
   (add a prepositional phrase) they ran
   _____
   (add a prepositional phrase) to earn money
   _____.
   (add a prepositional phrase)

d) They gave _____
   (add a direct object)
   _____.
   (add a prepositional phrase)

e) They gave _____
   (add a direct object)
   _____
   (add a prepositional phrase)
   _____.
   (add a prepositional phrase)

THE NOUN RESTATEMENT

EXERCISE 17

What is a noun restatement?

_____

_____

EXERCISE 18

Write three sentences that demonstrate noun restatements that follow the nouns they restate. In each sentence, underline all the noun restatements. Draw an arrow to the noun or pronoun that is renamed.

EXAMPLE: The mayor owns a house in my neighborhood, the big, green <u>house</u>.

a) _____

_____

b) _____

_____

c) _____

_____

THE NOUN RESTATEMENT

EXERCISE 19

What is a subject restatement?

_____

_____

_____

EXERCISE 20

Write three sentences that contain subject restatements. In each sentence, underline all the subject restatements. Draw an arrow to the noun or pronoun that is renamed.

EXAMPLE: Someday, a woman will be <u>President</u> of the United States.

a) _____

b) _____

c) _____

THE NOUN RESTATEMENT

EXERCISE 21

In the following sentences, underline all the noun restatements. Draw an arrow to the noun or pronoun that is renamed by a noun restatement.

EXAMPLE: Your friend will soon be here with her brother, <u>Darius</u>.

a) I received a wonderful gift from my parents, the computer I wanted.

b) My sister is learning to speak Norwegian which is my grandparents' first language.

c) Lewis and Clark traveled to the Pacific Ocean and one of the oldest towns in Oregon, Astoria.

d) When they visited Beijing, they were most amazed by the Forbidden City, the former Imperial Palace of China.

THE NOUN RESTATEMENT

EXERCISE 22

In the following sentences, underline all the noun restatements, including subject restatements. Draw an arrow to the noun or pronoun that is renamed by a noun restatement.

EXAMPLE OF SUBJECT RESTATEMENT:

He is going to be a <u>senior</u> this year.

a) The girls were looking forward to the Winter Ball, the first formal dance of the year.

b) School dances are the best social activities we have.

c) Some of our regular dances are the Welcome Dance and the Sweetheart's Ball.

d) My favorite school dance is the Prom, which is held in the spring just before Commencement.

e) Albert Einstein's parents were Hermann and Pauline Einstein.

f) Abraham Lincoln became the sixteenth U.S. President even though he was once an unknown lawyer from Illinois.

g) Some forms of Chinese art are the finest of any in the world.

h) During the Shang Dynasty in China, bronze cups and pots were crafted that were the most intricate examples of Bronze Age art in the world.

VERBS CAN ACT AS NOUNS

EXERCISE 23

Complete each sentence with a form of the verb given by filling the blank in a way that makes sense.

a) Horseback _____ (ride) is a fantastic way to explore the countryside.

b) Should you cancel _____ (leave) today because of the snow?

c) Emmanuel refused _____ (guess) the answers to questions he didn't know.

d) We were trying _____ (find) a job together.

e) Martin and Aliyah loved _____ (ski) best on tree-lined ski slopes.

f) I have wanted_____ (play) football professionally for years.

FINAL EXERCISE

FINAL EXERCISE 24

In the sentences below, do the following:
- label every noun or pronoun that is the subject of a sentence with an S.
- label every noun or pronoun that is a direct object with D.O. and those that are indirect objects with I.O.
- underline every prepositional phrase and label the noun or pronoun that is the object of the preposition with O.P.
- double underline all the noun restatements, including subject restatements. Draw an arrow to the noun or pronoun that is renamed by a noun restatement.

a) Our high school choir won first place in the state competition!

b) This has never happened before.

c) This win was the result of years of hard work.

d) First our music director, who is an excellent musician, gave each student an audition and chose the best singers to be in the choir.

e) Then, he chose an assortment of music that displayed our versatility.

f) After months of rehearsals, the music director gave some students solos to sing.

g) They also practiced the reading of music for the competition.

h) After many more rehearsals and performances, the choir was the best it had ever been.

FINAL EXERCISE

FINAL EXERCISE 25

In the sentences below, do the following:
- label every noun or pronoun that is the subject of a sentence with an S.
- label every noun or pronoun that is a direct object with D.O. and those that are indirect objects with I.O.
- underline every prepositional phrase and label the noun or pronoun that is the object of the preposition with O.P.
- double underline all the noun restatements, including subject restatements. Draw an arrow to the noun or pronoun that is renamed by a noun restatement.

a) I like making all kinds of art. My brother, Giovanni, only likes computers.

b) He can program a computer and build one.

c) He has given me lessons on how to do simple computer programming.

d) My favorite art form is pottery, but I'm still learning about it.

e) Eventually, I may be making fine pottery like the vases made in many East Asian countries.

f) When I finish a pot now, I put my special symbol, a spiral, on the bottom.

g) I made a special pottery sculpture for my parents and gave it to them last year.

PART 6
WHAT IS CASE?

WHAT IS CASE?

EXERCISE 1

What does case mean in grammar?

_____

_____

_____

THE POSSESSIVE CASE

EXERCISE 2

What is the possessive case?

_____

_____

_____

_____

THE POSSESSIVE CASE

EXERCISE 3

Make up two sentences using nouns in the possessive case.

a) _____

b) _____

EXERCISE 4

Make up four sentences using pronouns in the possessive case.

a) _____

b) _____

c) _____

d) _____

THE POSSESSIVE CASE

EXERCISE 5

Read the story below, and underline the nouns and pronouns in the possessive case.

Annika and <u>her</u> brother, Sven, were picking blueberries in <u>their town's</u> meadow. It was starting to get dark. Sven thought he had enough berries to make a pie, but Annika said, "Let's pick some more. I don't have enough for <u>mine</u>."

Suddenly, they heard something crashing through the forest. <u>Sven's</u> eyes grew big when he recognized that he was looking at a bear. He tapped <u>Annika's</u> shoulder and motioned to her to be still. She froze instantly. Slowly they backed into the bushes, hoping <u>their</u> movements would not be detected. <u>Hers</u> were not noticed. <u>His</u> were.

THE NOMINATIVE CASE

EXERCISE 6

What is the nominative case?

_____

_____

_____

EXERCISE 7

Make up six sentences with different pronouns in the nominative case.

a) _____

_____

b) _____

_____

c) _____

_____

THE NOMINATIVE CASE

d) _____

_____

e) _____

_____

f) _____

_____

EXERCISE 8

Choose the nominative form of pronoun in each of the following sentences.

a) My brother and _____ (me, I) both play the piano.

b) _____ (Her, She) and her friends compete at chess.

c) _____ (Us, We), the seniors, pledge to make this the most productive school year of our lives.

d) Who planned that event? _____ (Them, They) did.

e) Avi usually plays tennis better than _____ (I, me) do.

f) Who wrote that play? It was _____ (he, him).

THE NOMINATIVE CASE

EXERCISE 9

Read each sentence to see if the pronoun used is in the nominative case. If a different pronoun is needed, cross out the incorrect one and write the correct one above it.

a) Rafaella and me are twins.

b) Raoul and myself are both on the varsity team.

c) Whom did all this work? It was me.

d) Who is there? It is her.

e) Mochi writes better essays than me.

THE OBJECTIVE CASE

EXERCISE 10

What is the objective case?

_____
_____
_____

EXERCISE 11

Make up six sentences with different pronouns in the objective case.

a) _____
_____
_____

b) _____
_____
_____

c) _____
_____
_____

THE OBJECTIVE CASE

d) _____

e) _____

f) _____

EXERCISE 12

Choose the objective form of pronoun in each of the following sentences.

a) Is that gift for _____ (me, I)?

b) The coach gave Hari and _____ (he, him) new basketballs to use.

c) The teacher asked Deshaun and _____ (her, she) to start the discussion.

d) The chess team won their tournament! It was a challenging match for _____ (they, them).

THE OBJECTIVE CASE

e) It was an important milestone for _____ (we, us).

f) I think you should give the assignment to _____ (I, me).

g) To _____ (who, whom) did you give that role in the play?

h) Do you know who can unlock the cabinet for _____ (we, us)?

i) My father gave my brother and _____ (I, me) spending money.

j) _____ (Who, Whom) is the special dinner for?

EXERCISE 13

Read each sentence to see if the pronoun used is in the objective case. If a different pronoun is needed, cross out the incorrect one and write the correct one above it.

a) The candy is for myself.

b) Our grandmother gave Mateo and I our gifts early.

c) Abeni and Abeo are sisters from Nigeria who are coming to visit we.

d) The best soccer player will be he.

e) People were waiting at the food bank until food could be served to they.

f) For who are you waiting?

THE OBJECTIVE CASE

EXERCISE 14

Write the correct form of pronoun in the blanks.

a) The boys and _____ are going snowboarding.

b) I saw _____ over by the baseball field.

c) It was _____ who decorated the room.

d) You and _____ can do it by ourselves.

e) The job was given to _____ and _____.

f) _____ and her sister were here yesterday.

g) _____ is coming to dinner?

h) I can't wait to see Amol _____ I haven't seen in a year.

i) _____ students are happy with the schedule change.

j) The teachers gave awards to those of _____ who worked hard all month.

FINAL EXERCISE 15

Read each sentence to see if the pronoun used is in the correct case. If a different pronoun is needed, cross out the incorrect one and write the correct one above it.

a) My sister and her both took violin lessons.

b) Mikhail and myself will be happy to explain that.

c) The bus driver picked up Larissa and she.

d) All of us students researched that current event.

e) Who would lend my roommate and I a dollar?

f) The students' video had a section about Manuel and me.

g) The children's room was decorated for their birthday.

h) Both Pierre and him were given parts in the play.

i) My mother made dinner for my friends and I.

j) Whom is doing the cover artwork?

k) It was me.

l) My grandfather is the one person for who I would change my schedule.

EXERCISE ANSWERS

Part 1—Nouns And Pronouns 159

Part 2—Verbs 169

Part 3—Other Parts Of Speech 179

Part 4—The Sentence 193

Part 5—Jobs Nouns And Pronouns Do In Sentences 199

Part 6—What Is Case? 207

PART 1
NOUNS AND PRONOUNS

GRAMMAR

1. Responses will vary.

SENTENCES & PARTS OF SPEECH

2. A sentence is a group of words that expresses a *complete thought*.

3. Answers will vary.

NOUNS

4. Nouns are words that name a person, place, thing or idea.

5. Common nouns name a general type of thing

6. Answers will vary.

7. Proper nouns name a particular person, place, or thing.

8. Answers will vary.

9. a) Some <u>boys</u> want to be <u>firefighters</u> when they grow up.

   b) <u>Lucas</u> did, and he knew he would have to be very strong to pass the physical <u>test</u> required to become a <u>firefighter</u>.

   c) He trained hard and knew he would be ready for the <u>test</u> when he was twenty-one.

   d) He wasn't as certain that he could rush into a burning <u>building</u> to bring a <u>person</u> to <u>safety</u>.

   e) Ten <u>years</u> later, he was a <u>firefighter</u> in <u>Salem</u>, <u>Oregon</u> and found all the <u>courage</u> he needed to go into a burning <u>house</u> and rescue two <u>people</u>.

10. Answers will vary.

NOUNS AND PRONOUNS

PRONOUNS

11. A pronoun is a word that *takes the place of a noun*.

12. We use pronouns so we don't need to repeat the names of things over and over.

13. Personal pronouns are used instead of the name of a person or a thing.

14. Possessive pronouns are a type of personal pronoun that show ownership. Example sentence will vary.

15. a) <u>We</u> were amazed to see how well Sadie, the new girl, played tennis.

    b) <u>She</u> had been playing tennis since <u>she</u> was five years old and <u>she</u> had had excellent coaches.

    c) <u>They</u> had taught <u>her</u> how to play tennis like a professional.

    d) First prize in every tournament had been <u>hers</u> since <u>she</u> had been twelve years old.

    e) One day <u>she</u> lost her special, purple tennis racket. Her parents found one and asked her if it was <u>hers</u>.

16. Note: Any noun or pronoun that makes sense and communicates clearly can be accepted.

    a) She congratulated him (add a personal pronoun)

    b) That car is mine. (add a possessive pronoun)

    c) They gave us (add a personal pronoun) many treats. (add a noun)

    d) The teacher told him (add a personal pronoun) to rewrite the paper because his (add a possessive pronoun) was poorly written the first time.

17. Note: The pronouns below are the ones intended. However, any personal or possessive pronoun that makes sense and communicates clearly can be accepted.

    a) Let me tell you about our school trip to Europe.

NOUNS AND PRONOUNS

b) After flying all night to London, **we** had to find our own luggage and carry **it** through the airport. My sister wasn't sure which suitcase was **hers**.

c) **We** were very tired, but our tour guide insisted that **we** walk around London all day to stay awake.

d) Finally after dinner, **we** returned to our hotel.

e) Our luggage had been all mixed up, so **we** spent an hour sorting **it** out.

f) Our guide would hold up a suitcase and ask, "Whose is this?" The owner would say, "That is **mine**."

g) Then **he/she** would take **it** and go to **his/her** room to sleep.

h) The next day, **we** were well rested and enjoyed seeing some beautiful parts of England.

18. Reflexive pronouns refer back to someone or something in the sentence.

19. Answers will vary but should contain one of these reflexive pronouns:

    myself   *yourself*   *himself*   *herself*   *oneself*
    itself   *ourselves*   *yourselves* *themselves*

20. Note: The pronouns below are the ones intended. However, any reflexive pronoun that makes sense and communicates clearly can be accepted.

    a) In the dining room, she poured **herself** a drink to go with her meal.

    b) The deer healed **itself** by licking its wound.

    c) The students fixed **themselves** a snack before studying at night.

    d) Every year, we treated **ourselves** to a French dinner on our birthday.

    e) I **myself** locked every door last night.

21. Demonstrative means showing. Demonstrative pronouns show or point out someone or something.

22. Answers will vary.

NOUNS AND PRONOUNS

23. Note: The pronouns below are the ones intended. However, any demonstrative pronoun that makes sense and communicates clearly can be accepted.

    a) I never thought he would do <u>that</u>.

    b) <u>This</u> is Mary's room.

    c) Who owns <u>these</u>?

    d) <u>This</u> belongs to Mary and <u>that</u> belongs to Martin.

24. Interrogative pronouns are used in place of a noun when asking a question.

25. Answers will vary.

26. a) <u>Who</u> is your favorite coach?

    b) <u>Which</u> computer should I buy?

    c) Why don't you come to the movies with us? (*Why* is not a pronoun.)

    d) To <u>whom</u> should I send this letter?

    e) <u>What</u> did you say to her?

    f) How did you do that? (*How* is not a pronoun.)

    g) <u>Which</u> countries have you visited?

    h) <u>Who</u> is the new photography instructor?

27. Note: The pronouns below are the ones intended. However, any demonstrative pronoun that makes sense and communicates clearly can be accepted.

    This is a story about my dog, Jemma. One day **we** were walking in a field when **she** spotted something and ran off across the field. **I** ran after **her** but had soon exhausted **myself.**

    "**What** am I going to do? **Who** should **I** go to?" **I** thought.

    I started by going to a farmhouse on the far side of the field.

    A woman opened the door and Jemma was standing next to **her.**

Jemma furiously wagged her tail when **she** saw **me** and the woman asked, "Is **this** your dog?"

"Yes, **she** is **mine**, I said.

The woman told **me** that Jemma found her new puppy that had been lost in the field and brought **it** to **her**.

She was so grateful that **she** gave Jemma a steak to eat!

28. Relative pronouns relate a descriptive group of words to a noun or pronoun mentioned earlier.

29. Answers will vary, but one of these relative pronouns should be used within each sentence:

    who   *whom*   *which*   *what*   *that*

30. a) I learned about biology in the course <u>that</u> I just finished.

    b) The teacher <u>who</u> taught me writing knew more about using language than anyone else I know.

    c) You can borrow my dictionary, <u>which</u> is on the bookshelf above my desk.

    d) Don't ask for <u>whom</u> I am making this dress; it is a secret.

    e) The children <u>who</u> discovered the cave made it their secret meeting place.

    f) The apprenticeship was <u>what</u> I needed to gain better organizational skills.

    g) The coach <u>who</u> taught our team how to work together led us to the championship.

    h) My last year in school, <u>which</u> was the most challenging, was the best preparation for my career.

    i) Anna is the student <u>who</u> is managing this project.

    j) That teacher taught me math in a way <u>that</u> helped me really understand it.

NOUNS AND PRONOUNS

31. a) Alexander Graham Bell is the man for <u>whom</u> many telephone companies were named.

   b) The Tulip Festival, <u>which</u> takes place in April, has flowers of all colors of the rainbow.

   c) Brioche is a slightly sweet, egg bread <u>that</u> I could eat all day.

   d) That computer is broken, but it will be fixed by tomorrow. (No relative pronoun. In this sentence *that* is a demonstrative pronoun.)

   e) This protein shake is exactly <u>what</u> I need before exercising.

   f) To prepare the dinner, the chef cooked the main dish and vegetables first and the dessert last. (No relative pronoun.)

   g) Annie is the girl <u>who</u> oversees the project, so talk to her about helping with it.

   h) There is an expensive jacket in lost and found. To <u>whom</u> does it belong?

   i) The art project <u>that</u> won a national award will be displayed at the art show tomorrow.

   j) Who is going on the field trip next week? (No relative pronoun. In this sentence *who* is an interrogative pronoun.)

   k) Everyone on the committee promised to do one job, but now they have forgotten <u>what</u> they promised to do.

   l) What should we do about it? (No relative pronoun. In this sentence *what* is an interrogative pronoun.)

32. Note: The pronouns below are the ones intended. However, any personal or possessive pronoun that makes sense and communicates clearly can be accepted.

   a) The high school students put on a play <u>that</u> was performed in May.

   b) He was the student <u>who</u> earned a place on the Dean's List.

   c) My friend for <u>whom</u> I bought this gift turns sixteen tomorrow.

   d) The school supplies <u>that</u> we bought in September are gone now.

NOUNS AND PRONOUNS

    e) The sweet, warm cocoa was precisely **what** they wanted on a cold, snowy day.

    f) We handed our boarding passes to the flight attendant **who** invited us to board the plane.

    g) She did well on the test because it was exactly **what** she had expected.

    h) Our yearbook, **which** went on sale today, had a beautiful cover this year.

    i) My teachers are people for **whom** I will always be grateful.

    j) Jupiter, **which** the largest planet of our solar system, helps protect Earth from asteroids.

33. Indefinite pronouns refer generally to people or things without naming the exact one.

34. Answers will vary.

35. a) <u>Everyone</u> on the track team will be competing in the meet next month.

    b) The coach really hopes that <u>nobody</u> is ill that day.

    c) <u>Several</u> of the boys on the relay team have world-class speed.

    d) <u>No one</u> on the girls' team has that top speed but <u>some</u> come very close.

    e) As a unit, the girls' relay team can beat the <u>others</u> in the meet.

    f) The hurdles challenge <u>everybody</u> who competes in that race.

    g) <u>All</u> of the athletes' parents will cheer for them during the competition.

    h) <u>Somebody</u> dressed as the school mascot cheered with the crowd.

36. a) My mother baked enough cupcakes for <u>everyone</u> at the party to have two.

    b) <u>Several</u> of the boys wanted to eat many more than two. (*Many* is an adjective not a pronoun in this sentence.)

NOUNS AND PRONOUNS

    c) A few girls didn't want their cupcakes, so they gave them to the boys. (No indefinite pronoun. *Few* is an adjective not a pronoun in this sentence.)

    d) The party started in the beach house, but <u>somebody</u> asked if they could go swimming.

    e) Then the party quickly became a beach party that <u>everybody</u> enjoyed in different ways.

    f) A <u>few</u> of the boys were swimming and diving in the waves.

    g) <u>Some</u> of the girls sat on blankets and soaked up the sun.

    h) Several people walked along the beach picking up seashells. (No indefinite pronoun. *Several* is an adjective not a pronoun in this sentence.)

    i) It was so much fun that <u>many</u> of my guests stayed all day.

37. Note: The pronouns below are the ones intended. However, any indefinite pronoun that makes sense and communicates clearly can be accepted.

    a) As guests arrived at her birthday party, Emily asked if they would like **something** to eat or drink.

    b) Emily knew **someone** had baked her a birthday cake, but she didn't know who.

    c) **Anyone** who brought a gift received a special thank you.

    d) Emily made sure that **nobody** left the party hungry.

    e) At the end of her party, Emily thanked **everyone** for coming.

38. Answers will vary. Ensure words labeled as indefinite pronoun words are used as pronouns, not as modifiers.

FINAL EXERCISES

39. Note: The nouns below are the ones intended. However, any noun that makes sense and communicates clearly can be accepted.

NOUNS AND PRONOUNS

a) Last *summer* [common], my family and I went on *vacation* [common].

b) We rented a *house* [common] at the beach in the state of *Oregon* [proper].

c) We swam in the *ocean* [common] and played beach volleyball for *hours* [common].

d) My sister, *Christine* [proper], and I both loved riding *horses* [common] on the beach.

e) It was the best *vacation* [common] ever!

40. Note: The pronouns below are the ones intended. However, any pronoun that makes sense and communicates clearly should be accepted.

   a) This August **we** backpacked through the mountains of the western United States on a section of the Pacific Crest Trail.

   b) **This** is **one** of the most beautiful hiking trails in America **that** extends from Canada to Mexico.

   c) **We** had to carry **all** of the supplies **we** needed in our backpacks while walking from southern Washington State to northern California.

   d) There were stations along the trail where **we** could resupply.

   e) At each station, **we** had to ask **ourselves**, "**What** will **we** need for the next 200 miles?"

   f) Along the trail, **we** made friends **who** came from all over the world.

   g) **One** of the best places was Edison Lake, high in the Sierra Nevada Mountains of California.

   h) **This** was an extraordinarily beautiful spot with a supply cabin at one end of the lake.

   i) **We** hope to return to **it** every year.

PART 2
VERBS

VERBS

1. A verb is a word that communicates action or being. It is the verb of a sentence that tells what is happening or existing.

2. Answers will vary.

3. Action verbs communicate about physical actions such as *run, walk, talk, jump* or *eat*, about mental actions such as *think, worry, consider,* and *remember*, and about possession such as *have, own, possess*.

4. Answers will vary.

5. A being verb is a word that tells what or how something is.

6. Answers will vary.

7. a) Soccer <u>is</u> (B) my favorite sport.

   b) I <u>played</u> (A) extensively for soccer teams last year.

   c) My last coach <u>said</u> (A) that I <u>had become</u> (B) an excellent player.

   d) All summer I <u>exercised</u> (A) to stay in top physical condition.

   e) In September, I <u>seemed</u> (B) much stronger so I <u>tried</u> (A) out for the varsity team.

   f) I <u>hope</u> (A) that I <u>make</u> (A) it!

8. Answers will vary but there should be some sentences with multiple verbs. For example, *She <u>will be writing</u> her second novel next year.* or *When writing, she <u>writes</u> then <u>revises</u> and <u>proofreads</u>.*

VERBS

9. a) Will you finish your work soon?

   b) We should be dressing and leaving for the concert in one hour.

   c) We will drive into the city and eat in a wonderful restaurant first.

   d) Then we will enjoy the spring performance of the symphony orchestra.

   e) I do not know all of the music on the program for the evening but will enjoy it.

   f) After the concert, we might use our backstage passes and meet all the musicians.

   g) Then we will stay in a five-star hotel for the night and drive home in the afternoon.

TRANSITIVE AND INTRANSITIVE VERBS

10. A transitive verb is an action verb that communicates an action, ownership or result happening to a direct object. A transitive verb always has a direct object.

11. Answers will vary but will use *take*, *own* and *believe*.

12. An intransitive verb is a verb that simply communicates that the action or existence occurs. That means an intransitive verb never has a direct object. Being verbs never have direct objects, so they are always intransitive.

13. Answers will vary but will use *catch*, *ride* and *laugh*.

VERBS

14. a) Next month, I <u>can take</u> the (test) for a driving permit.

    b) I <u>have planned</u> my driving (lessons) so they are gradually more difficult.

    c) I <u>will drive</u> my mother's (car) mostly and <u>practice</u> with her.

    d) On my first lesson, I <u>backed</u> into a ditch at the roadside.

    e) That <u>was</u> embarrassing!

    f) After that, I <u>backed</u> up more slowly.

    g) As I <u>mastered</u> each driving (skill), I <u>became</u> a good driver.

    h) After six months, I <u>could take</u> my final driving (test) and I <u>passed</u> (it.)

15. Answers will vary slightly. The first verb is transitive. The second is intransitive.

16. Answers will vary.

17. Answers will vary.

18. Answers will vary.

SUBJECT-VERB AGREEMENT

19. a) Jack (work, <u>works</u>) out the solution to the problem.

    b) Can you (<u>bring</u>, brings) a cake to the picnic?

    c) Jessica and Jill (learns, <u>learn</u>) many new things each year.

    d) The volleyball team (<u>plays</u>, play) the champions next week.

    e) Nobody (write, <u>writes</u>) music as well as you.

    f) Several of my friends (<u>ski</u>, skis) in Colorado every winter.

    g) None of our teammates (<u>score</u>, scores) more goals than you.

    h) Each of them (<u>gets</u>, get) a new backpack.

    i) Someone (<u>is</u>, are) driving to the city tomorrow.

    j) Both of the cakes (tastes, <u>taste</u>) great.

    k) All of my schoolwork (take, <u>takes</u>) time to do.

VERBS

l) Everyone in all the states (vote, <u>votes</u>) in November.

m) Some of the others (<u>leave</u>, leaves) for Asia in the morning.

n) Any of those sports (seems, <u>seem</u>) like fun.

o) Most of the berry pie (have, <u>has</u>) been eaten.

p) Neither of us (<u>qualifies</u>, qualify) for the final swim race.

20. a) Robert or Ethan are riding with me. is

b) Each of the games take two hours to play. takes

c) Grasses and a certain type of moss covers the forest floor. cover

d) All of my songs is saved in my tablet. are

e) Everyone with passports are in this line. is

f) A computer, pencil, and eraser is required for that class. are

g) Either of those paths are the correct one to take. is

h) Some of my brothers are here. OK

i) Several of the stars in the Milky Way Galaxy are red giants. OK

j) Everybody in the gym were surprised at the game's score. was

k) Most of my work require specialized knowledge. requires

l) Anabelle or her friends plans to decorate the hall. plan

THE FOUR FORMS OF VERBS

21. a) Infinitive: (to) talk

Present participle: talking

Past: talked

Past participle: (have) talked

VERBS

  b) Infinitive: (to) choose

  Present participle: choosing

  Past: chose

  Past participle: (have) chosen

22. Sentences may vary but not the verb forms shown in bold.

  a) *come*

  (present participle) Today I am coming home at 5 p.m.

  (past) Yesterday I came home.

  (past participle) Often in the past I have come home for the holidays.

  b) *do*

  (infinitive) Today I chose to do my online courses.

  or

  I do twenty exercises every morning.

  (present participle) Today we are doing the second scene of the play.

  (past) Yesterday I did all my assignments on time.

  (past participle) Often I have done my homework early in the morning.

  c) *give*

  (present participle) Today I am giving two piano lessons in the evening.

  (past) Yesterday I gave a donation to the school.

  (past participle) For several years I have given French lessons.

  d) *know* or *throw*

  (infinitive)

  Today I am going to know if I have been accepted to college.
   or
  Today, I want to throw the first pitch in the baseball game.

VERBS

(present participle)

Today he **is throwing** the ball poorly.
   or
The trick is **knowing** when your artwork is complete.

(past)

Yesterday I **knew** the answer.
   or
Yesterday he **threw** the ball very well.

(past participle)

Often I **have known** the right thing to say, but not today.
   or
Often he **has thrown** the ball too hard.

VERB TENSES

23. a) Sean **speaks** French fluently.

    b) Our neighbors **walk** to the park every day.

    c) The phases of our moon **cause** the tides.

    d) Elise **takes** her final exam today.

    e) We always **eat** lunch at noon.

    f) Nurses **care** for sick people.

    g) He **wakes** up at 7:00 every morning.

24. Answers will vary.

25. a) We **went** to see a great play last week. (go)

    b) The play **was** a very good comedy. (be)

    c) **Did** you **see** it too? (do/see)

    d) Yes, we **saw** it two days ago. (see)

    e) The actors **performed** their comedic roles very well. (perform)

VERBS

    f) After the play, we **ate** dinner at a new restaurant. (eat)

    g) **Wasn't** that too late to eat dinner? (be/not)

    h) Not at all, we **relaxed** over a light meal and **discussed** the play. (relax/discuss)

    i) We **did not like** to get home too early. (do/not/like)

26. Answers will vary.

27. The verb used may vary but all verbs should be in the future tense.

    a) Her friends asked her, "Where **shall** we **eat** lunch?

    b) Wait for me. It **won't take/will not take** me long to get ready.

    c) I **will be** ready for the dance in ten minutes.

    d) She asked her mother, **Shall** I **put** the vase of flowers on the dining room table?

    e) He loves that restaurant and **won't eat/will not eat** anywhere else.

    f) Let's go to the movies. What **shall** we **see**?

    g) Do you think you **will join** that team next spring?

    h) Our soccer team **will** probably **play** that opponent in the championship game next week.

    i) Next November, I **will** probably **write** a short novel.

    j) I'm going to that party tomorrow. Do you think you **will go**?

    k) Janice is worried that she **won't finish** her paintings in time for the art show.

    l) I'm sure Kyle **will keep** his promise.

28. Answers will vary.

VERBS

29.
         pron.   v.   v.   n.   n.
a) She will study biology in college.

         n.   v.   n.   n.   n.
b) My family takes a vacation in Hawaii every year.

         n.   v.   n.   n.
c) John wrote a short novel last summer.

         n.   v.   n.   n.
d) Joyce bought a new dress for the dance.

         v.   pron.   v.   n.
e) Are you going to the volleyball game?

FINAL EXERCISES

30. a) Last week, we swim at the beach. swam

b) Last night, temperatures go below freezing so the fountain freezes. went, froze

c) It costed ten dollars to go to the school dance. cost

d) They has a meeting today. had

e) He began playing soccer ten years ago. OK

f) In the past, we have drunk well water, but now we <u>drank</u> bottled water. drink

   Note: We *have drunk* well water.... is correct.

g) Sara takes her final exam last week. took

h) My mother has knowed her best friend for forty-five years. known

i) Last month, Jill feels so happy when she travelled to meet her friends from high school. felt

j) Jason ran a four-minute mile yesterday. OK

k) I brang a pie to my family's holiday feast. brought

l) Shelly written a letter to her U.S. Senator about an unfair law, and it be changed.   wrote, was

31. a) Everyone is going (go, present) to the volleyball game today.   goes/

b) Next month, Jennifer and Sierra will be (be, future) on their way to Europe.

c) When I was 4 years old, I began (begin, past) taking dance lessons.

d) Every year, each of the students takes (take, present) on difficult community projects. Note: *Each* is the subject of this sentence, not *students*. It is a singular pronoun and *takes* the singular verb takes, not take (plural).

e) This year, both my sisters are studying (study, present) at the colleges of their choice.   study/

f) James drank (drink, past) water with minerals before every soccer game.

g) All the students sang (sing, past) well in the choir performance.

h) Because they had practiced so hard, they knew (know, past) they would do well in the competition.

i) I brought (bring, past) snacks to the Student Council meeting.

j) We wrote (write, past) over ten essays in the past few months.

PART 3
OTHER PARTS OF SPEECH

ADJECTIVES

1. An adjective modifies a noun or pronoun. It usually answers one of these questions: *which?*, *how many?*, *what kind of?*.

2. Answers will vary.

3. The only articles are *a*, *an* and *the*. Articles answer both *which?* and *how many?*. For *a* and *an*, the answer to *how many?* is always one. *The* answers the question *which?*, because it specifies the particular person or thing named.

4. Answers will vary.

5. Answers will vary.

6. Answers will vary.

7. a) <u>The</u> day in <u>early</u> May was <u>sunny</u> and <u>breezy</u>.
       art.   adj.   adj.   adj.

   b) We enjoyed <u>a</u> <u>delicious</u> dinner at <u>the</u> <u>French</u> restaurant.
                  art. adj.   art. adj.

   c) I suggest you buy <u>that</u> <u>small</u> computer you found in <u>the</u> <u>local</u> newspaper.
                       adj. adj.   art. adj.

   d) <u>That</u> <u>Arabian</u> horse climbs <u>those</u> <u>mountain</u> trails easily.
      adj.   adj.   adj.   adj.

   e) Which of <u>the</u> <u>chocolate</u> cupcakes are <u>gluten-free</u>?
             art. adj.   adj.

OTHER PARTS OF SPEECH

8. Answers will vary.

9. a)   art. adj. n.   v. art. adj.   n.
   A lemon cake makes a perfect dessert.

   b)   pron. v. adj.   n.   art. adj.   n.
   She found that reference in the school library.

   c)   adj. adj. n.   art. n.   v. adj.
   Those fir trees behind the building are ancient.

   d)   pron. v.   v.   adj.   n.   adj. n.
   I am studying two languages this year.

   e)   v. pron. v. pron. art. adj. adj. n.
   Can you meet me in the old, science lab?

ADVERBS

10. a) An adverb modifies a verb or another modifier and it usually answers one of these questions: *how?*, *when?*, *where?* or *to what extent?*.

    b) Answers will vary.

11. a) Zack sprinted <u>easily</u> across the field.

    b) The raccoon climbed the tree <u>carefully</u>.

    c) He will <u>soon</u> be sixteen years old.

    d) She runs <u>better</u> in the morning and <u>really</u> hates evening competitions.

    e) Your dress is a <u>beautiful</u> red color.

    f) These are <u>extraordinarily</u> delicious cookies.

g) That <u>dark</u> red horse is <u>much</u> taller than she is.

h) The <u>deep</u> blue sky against the <u>brilliant</u> white clouds accentuated all the colors of the landscape.

i) Zack reads <u>very</u> accurately.

j) My new computer runs <u>much</u> faster than I expected.

k) I have never seen such an <u>amazingly</u> <u>deep</u> blue sky.

l) John writes French <u>very</u> quickly and reads it <u>even</u> faster.

m) I <u>really</u> appreciate your <u>completely</u> honest answer.

n) We drove <u>past</u> many, <u>bright</u> green fields in Oregon this spring.

12. a) Mary walked slowly up the road. *or* Mary slowly walked up the road.
    b) Jack will soon be turning eighteen years old. *or* Soon, Jack will be turning eighteen years old.
    c) Quickly put away your books.
    d) The gray house became hot in the summer.
    e) I gladly gave her new clothes for work.

OTHER PARTS OF SPEECH

          pron. adv.   v.   adv. adj.   n.   adj.   n.

13. a) They always sailed across the deep blue Pacific every summer.

        adv.   adj.   n.   v.   adv.   adj. n.

   b) Happily, the whole family snowboarded well during that visit to

      n.

   Mt. Hood.

        v. pron. adv.   v.   adj.   n.

   c) Did you really write an adventure novel?

       pron.   v.   adv.   adv.   adj.   n.   adj. n.

   d) I   attended an incredibly useful soccer camp last fall.

        n.   v.   n.   adv.   adv.

   e) Anna serves a volleyball blazingly fast.

       pron. v.   adv.   pron. adj.   adj.   n.

   f) He runs faster than everyone else on the track team.

        adj.   n.   v. adv. adj.

   g) French food tastes so good.

         n.   v.   n.   adv.

   h) The chef tasted the sauce twice.

COMPARISON

14. a) Which do you like (<u>more</u>, most), coffee or tea?

   b) The weather is (more better, best, <u>better</u>) than yesterday.

   c) He is the (less, <u>least</u>) talkative of the three friends.

   d) That book was the (easier, most easy, <u>easiest</u>) of all the books on that level.

   e) The beach camping trip was (most wonderful, wonderfuler, <u>more wonderful</u>) than our other summer trip to the mountains.

OTHER PARTS OF SPEECH

    f) John is the (taller, most tall, <u>tallest</u>) of the three brothers.

    g) My puppy is (<u>more</u>, most, much) intelligent than her sister.

    h) She always likes to play music (more loudly, <u>louder</u>, the loudest) than her roommate.

15. Answers will vary.

MODIFIERS MADE FROM VERBS

16. A participle is formed by adding *–ing* or *–ed* to the basic form of a verb.

    A participle can be used two ways:

    1. as an adjective

    2. with some form of *be* or *have* to form a tense with two more verbs.

17. Answers will vary for both.

    An example sentence for the first one is:

        The *working* horse pulled plows and wagons for the farmer.

    An example sentence for the second one is:

        She has *worked* every night this week.

18. a) The <u>swimming</u> horse crossed the river easily. **horse**

    b) <u>Improved</u> by a new design, the house was remodeled in the summer. **house**

    c) Jane left the car <u>running</u> while she ran into the house to get something. **car**

    d) They were eager to hear the <u>visiting</u> professor's lecture. **professor**

    e) The <u>exhilarated</u> runner was the first to finish the race. **runner**

    f) The autumn leaves floated in the <u>swirling</u> wind. **wind**

    g) His <u>written</u> work is excellent. **work**

OTHER PARTS OF SPEECH

    h) The teacher helped his students with a specially planned algebra lesson. **lesson**

    i) In the fall, fish can hide under the leaves floating along the edge of the river. **leaves**

19. a) The haunted house frightened some people.

    b) The new mother calmed her crying baby.

    c) Samantha needed new riding clothes before her horseback riding competition.

    d) The students were very tired because they had studied late the night before.

    e) Women don't have voting rights everywhere in the world.

    f) Michael controlled the spinning ball and passed it to his teammate.

    g) Both biology and chemistry are evolving sciences.

    h) The seniors planned an exciting party for all the students.

    i) The stopped cars created a traffic jam.

    j) The choir gave an inspired, singing performance.

20. Answers will vary. The sentences given below are examples only. Any sentence that makes sense and has the participial phrase next to the noun or pronoun being modified, can be accepted.

    a) Singing as loud as possible, the soloist could be heard over the entire choir.

    b) Finding the solution to the problem, the student was proud of his work.

    c) Dancing and laughing the night away, the seniors celebrated their graduation.

    d) Guaranteed to be fresh, the vegetables in that store were superb.

    e) Thrilled to hear the good news, she congratulated her daughter on the new job.

    f) Written originally in French, the book was a masterpiece.

OTHER PARTS OF SPEECH

21. Answers will vary. The sentences given below are one correct solution. Any sentence that makes sense and has the participial phrase next to the noun or pronoun being modified can be accepted.

   a) Gazing into the mirror, she thought her dress looked perfect for the dance.

   b) Repaired and polished, my watch looked great when I picked it up from the jeweler.

   c) Invigorated from the hike, we welcomed some food and water when we returned home.

   d) Flying across the finish line, the cyclist won the race.

   e) After grazing the organic grass field, the farmer's cows were moved into the barn.

PREPOSITIONS

22. A preposition is a word that shows the relationship between a noun or pronoun following it and some other word(s) in the sentence.

23. Answers will vary.

24. a) Jamie walked <u>into</u> the field where his horse, Tolly, was grazing.

   b) Tolly ran <u>to</u> Jamie when he saw him.

   c) Then Jamie quickly saddled Tolly.

   d) They started riding <u>along</u> the edge <u>of</u> the forest.

   e) Suddenly, Jamie saw a small person scurry <u>behind</u> a fallen tree.

   f) Tolly sprinted <u>toward</u> the person and jumped <u>over</u> the fallen tree.

   g) Jamie turned fast and saw a forest gnome, who promptly disappeared!

25. a) Answers will vary.

   b) Answers will vary.

   c) Answers will vary.

OTHER PARTS OF SPEECH

26. a) <u>In 2017</u>, there was a total eclipse <u>of the sun</u> <u>in Oregon</u>.

    b) My friends and I prepared ahead <u>of time</u> and bought special glasses.

    c) These enabled us to look <u>at the sun</u> and protect our eyes <u>from damage</u>.

    d) To get the best view, we sat high <u>on a hill</u> <u>in a meadow</u>.

    e) As the moon's shadow fell <u>across the sun</u>, the bright summer morning grew darker and darker.

    f) When the moon had completely blocked the sun, the day turned <u>into a cool night</u> and the wind started to blow.

    g) Then the shadow moved <u>past the sun</u> and its rays gradually shone down <u>on us</u> again.

    h) Now, I fully appreciate the warmth and light <u>of our sun</u>.

27. a) The children's laughter <u>during the break</u> *(adj.)* was delightful.

    b) My grandmother always sat <u>in her favorite chair</u> *(adv.)*.

    c) Our campsite <u>beside the river</u> *(adj.)* was absolutely beautiful.

    d) Would you rather write <u>with a pen or pencil</u> *(adv.)*?

    e) This spring, we saw birds <u>of many kinds</u> *(adj.)*.

    f) My dog always gallops <u>to my side</u> *(adv.)* to greet me when I come home.

OTHER PARTS OF SPEECH

                              adv.
g) My grandfather painted <u>over one hundred watercolors</u>.

                  adv.   adv.
h) Our group hiked <u>through the forest</u> <u>to a waterfall</u>.

28. Answers will vary.

                    n.   v.   n. prep.
29. a) Our girls' volleyball team just won enough games for the

     n.   prep.   n. prep. n.
    district tournament in the fall of 2017.

            n.   v.   n. pron. v.   v. prep.
b) Their first opponent was a team they had already beaten in

    n.
    September.

   pron.   v.   n.   prep.   n.
c) They easily won that match in two hours.

      pron. v.   v.   n. pron. pron. v.
d) Next, they had to play a top-seeded school that they had never

    v.
    played before.

   prep.   n.   n.   v.   prep.   n.
e) Before that match, the team practiced late into the night.

      n.   v.   v. prep. n.   n.   v.
f) Their next game was filled with tension as the lead changed

    n.
    many times.

187

OTHER PARTS OF SPEECH

                n.   v.   v.   prep.   n.

g) Finally, our team triumphed and advanced to the State Championship.

      pron. prep.   n.   v.   pron. v. v. pron.

h) Everyone in our school was happy they had seen that.

CONJUNCTIONS

30. A conjunction is a word that joins other words or groups of words.

31. a) I would like to go to the play with you, but I don't have enough money.

    b) Do you want to play softball or run track this spring?

32. a) I would like to go to the concert, <u>but</u> I haven't earned enough money for the ticket.

    b) I have to study <u>so</u> I won't be able to go to the movies tonight.

    c) My mother does not ride horses <u>nor</u> does she ski, <u>but</u> all her daughters do. (*This sentence has two conjunctions.*)

    d) Would you like chicken <u>or</u> fish for dinner?

    e) The students learned to waltz <u>and</u> salsa before the school dance.

    f) Rigo is small, <u>yet</u> he is one of our best players.

    g) He spent his free time inventing new recipes, <u>for</u> he loved to delight people with new foods.

33. a) <u>Both</u> plums <u>and</u> peaches ripen in the summer.

    b) The children <u>either</u> played tag <u>or</u> swam all day.

    c) <u>Neither</u> Sam <u>nor</u> Ty like to play goalie.

    d) He <u>not only</u> studied French <u>but also</u> Chinese and Japanese.

    e) I didn't know <u>whether</u> she was joking <u>or</u> not.

    f) This dessert is <u>not only</u> sugar-free <u>but</u> it is <u>also</u> organic.

    g) This fall, you may choose to play <u>either</u> volleyball <u>or</u> soccer.

    h) <u>Both</u> the children <u>and</u> their parents learned a lot at the county fair.

OTHER PARTS OF SPEECH

34. a) <u>Until I walked through that forest</u>, I didn't understand its magic.

   b) I first noticed the butterflies of all colors <u>because there were hundreds of them</u>.

   c) I knew something was different <u>when I saw a butterfly land on a flower and make it grow</u>.

   d) <u>Before a butterfly touched a flower</u>, it had a normal blossom.

   e) <u>After a butterfly landed on a flower</u>, it grew four times the normal size with huge flowers.

   f) <u>As long as I stayed on the path</u>, I could enjoy the magic.

   g) Bad things happened <u>whenever I left the path</u>.

   h) <u>When I saw a flash of pure white and followed it off the path</u>, the wind howled and it started to rain.

   i) <u>Although I was frightened by the storm</u>, I continued to chase the white thing into a cave and was astonished to find a unicorn!

35. Sentences given below are examples. Answers will vary, but each sentence should contain at least one conjunction.

   a) I do not eat steak *and* potatoes.

   b) I would like to go to the movies, *but* I have too much work today.

   c) I always like to eat *either* fruits *or* vegetables at every meal.

   d) *Since* it was a sunny day, I went swimming at the beach.

   e) I never know *whether* to shake hands *or* give hugs when meeting someone.

   f) *Because* our team won, we celebrated with a pizza party.

   g) *When* it starts snowing, we will go skiing.

OTHER PARTS OF SPEECH

INTERJECTIONS

36. An interjection is a part of speech that is put between sentences or thoughts to express strong or sudden emotion. It is usually separate from a sentence and set off with an exclamation mark.

37. Wow! You have accomplished so much this year.

    Or similar sentences. Answers will vary.

FINAL EXERCISES

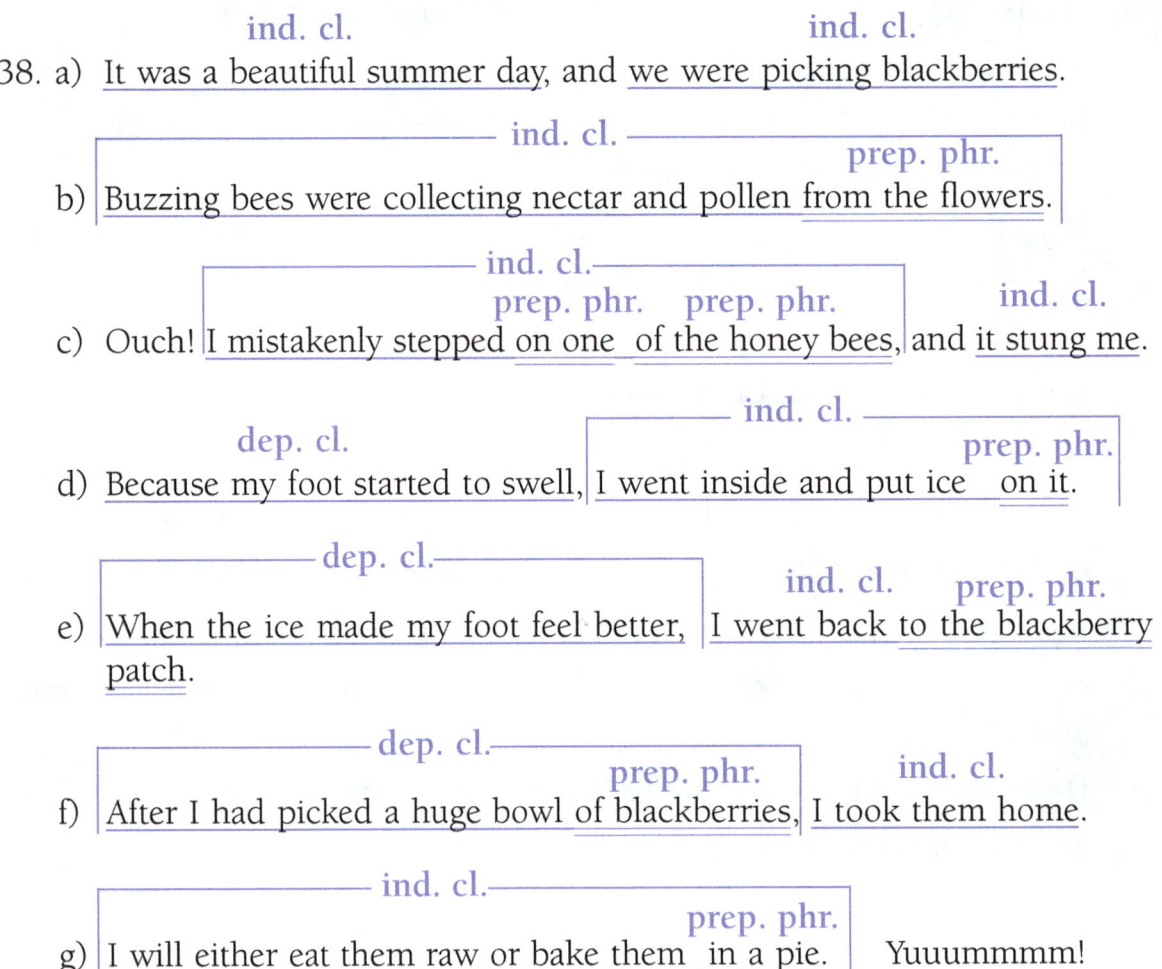

OTHER PARTS OF SPEECH

39.   pron. v. art. adj.   adj. n. conj. pron. v.   v.   n.
   a) It was a beautiful, summer day, and we were picking blackberries.

       adj.   n.   v.   v.   n.   conj. n. prep. art.   n.
   b) Buzzing bees were collecting nectar and pollen from the flowers.

      intj. pron. adv.   v.   prep. pron. prep. art. adj.   n.
   c) Ouch! I mistakenly stepped on one of the honey bees,

      conj. pron. v.   pron.
      and it stung me.

      conj. adj. n.   v.   v. pron. v.   adv.   conj. v.
   d) Because my foot started to swell, I went inside and put

      n. prep. pron.
      ice on it.

      conj. art. n.   v.   adj. n.   v.   adv.   pron. v.   adv.
   e) When the ice made my foot feel better, I went back

      prep. art.   adj.   n.
      to the blackberry patch.

      conj. pron. v.   v.   art. adj. n. prep.   n.   pron.
   f) After I had picked a huge bowl of blackberries, I

      v.   pron. adv.
      took them home.

      pron. v.   conj.   v. pron. adj. conj.   v.   pron. prep. art. n.   intj.
   g) I will either eat them raw or bake them in a pie. Yuuummmm!

PART 4
THE SENTENCE

THE SENTENCE

1. A sentence is a group of words that communicates a complete thought with a subject and its verb.

2. …a noun or pronoun that the sentence is about. Often there will be modifying words accompanying this noun or pronoun. This is the subject of the sentence.

3. Answers will vary.

4. Answers will vary.

5. A clause is a group of words that has a subject and its verb. There are two types of clauses, independent and dependent. Answers will vary on examples of a clause.

6. An independent clause expresses a complete thought and can stand alone as a sentence. Often, it is part of a bigger sentence.

7. A dependent clause has a subject and its verb but does not express a complete thought, so it leaves a person with a question.

8. Answers will vary.

9. Answers will vary.

10. a) Almost every weekend, <u>I</u> hike through the woods with my friends.

    b) <u>Jill</u> and <u>Susan</u> are going with me this weekend.

    c) <u>Jill</u> and <u>I</u> will be walking on the trails, but not Susan.

    d) <u>Susan</u> will run cross-country most likely and meet us at the lake.

    e) <u>She</u> walks with us for a little while, but <u>I</u> can see that she really wants to run.

    f) <u>I</u> tell her right away.

    g) <u>(You)</u> Go ahead and meet us later.

THE SENTENCE

    h) Where do you want to meet?

    i) We should meet at the lake by noon and eat a picnic lunch there.

11. a) Almost every weekend, I <u>hike</u> through the woods with my friends.

    b) Jill and Susan <u>are going</u> with me this weekend.

    c) Jill and I <u>will be walking</u> on the trails, but not Susan.

    d) Susan <u>will run</u> cross-country most likely and <u>meet</u> us at the lake.

    e) She <u>walks</u> with us for a little while, but I <u>can see</u> that she really wants to run.

    f) I <u>tell</u> her right away.

    g) (You) <u>Go</u> ahead and <u>meet</u> us later.

    h) Where <u>do</u> you <u>want</u> to meet?

    i) We <u>should meet</u> at the lake by noon and <u>eat</u> a picnic lunch there.

12. Answers will vary.

SENTENCE ERRORS

13. a) Since it is time to make my presentation and I've been ready for two weeks. fragment

    b) She laughed. complete

    c) Because Garrett loves to snowboard. fragment

    d) I don't know who the speaker is going to be today. complete

    e) Finish reading your book tonight. complete

    f) When I have written my novel and had it published. fragment

    g) As beautifully as they could sing. fragment

    h) All around the campus. fragment

14. a) He is reading a new book, it is about the American Revolution. run-on

    b) My favorite sport is volleyball because I like the teamwork. OK

c) Jeremy practices playing the guitar all the time, he plays for whoever will listen and asks their opinion of the song. **run-on**

d) On the track team, she sprinted and jumped hurdles and practiced relay races. **OK**

e) We sang together, my brother ate pizza, my mother ate a salad. **run-on**

f) During the holidays, I like cooking with my family and learning how to make new dishes. **OK**

g) We just got a new puppy, he needs a lot of training, we don't know what to name him. **run-on**

h) The weather was great the stadium had comfortable seats, our team was winning, it was a great day of watching the game. **run-on**

15. Answers will vary. The answers below are examples only. Any complete sentence that makes sense should be accepted.

    a) Since it is time to make my presentation and I've been ready for two weeks, **I'm not nervous at all.**

    b) Because Garrett loves to snowboard, **we go to the mountains every winter.**

    c) When I have written my novel and had it published, **I'd like to make an audiobook.**

    d) As beautifully as they could sing, **the concert was too long for my taste.**

    e) All around the campus, **the children ran and played.**

THE SENTENCE

16. Answers will vary. The answers below are examples only. Any run-on sentence that is revised into complete sentences and makes sense should be accepted.

   a) He is reading a new book. It is about the American Revolution.

   b) Jeremy practices playing the guitar all the time. He plays for whoever will listen and asks their opinion of the song.

   c) We sang together after my brother ate pizza and my mother ate a salad.

   d) We just got a new puppy. He needs a lot of training, and we don't know what to name him.

   e) The weather was great and the stadium had comfortable seats. Our team was winning, so it was a great day of watching the game.

THREE WAYS TO BUILD A SENTENCE

17. a) <u>As the days grow longer</u> (dep. cl.) <u>in the spring,</u> (prep phr.) <u>everything seems full</u> (Ind. cl.) <u>of life</u> (prep. phr.) <u>in the garden</u> (prep. phr.).

   b) <u>I'm planting flowers</u> (ind. cl.) <u>throughout the garden,</u> (prep. phr.) but <u>the boys are preparing the soil to plant vegetables</u> (ind. cl.) <u>in the back</u> (prep. phr.).

   c) <u>Since the mornings are still frosty</u> (dep. cl.) <u>in March,</u> (prep. phr.) <u>I can only plant flowers</u> (ind. cl.) <u>that can grow</u> (dep. cl.) <u>in the cold weather</u> (prep. phr.).

   d) <u>Most vegetables will have to wait</u> (ind. cl.) <u>until the weather warms up</u> (dep. cl.).

           dep. cl.   ind. cl.

e) <u>When it is April</u>, <u>we can plant all the flowers</u>.

          ind. cl.   prep. phr. prep. phr.

f) <u>We should plant all the vegetables</u> <u>before May</u> <u>at the latest</u>.

  prep. phr.   ind. cl.   dep. cl.

g) <u>In June</u>, <u>the sun can be so hot</u> <u>that all the plants need more water</u>.

      ind. cl.   prep. phr.

h) <u>The flowers are so pretty</u> <u>in May and June</u>.

        ind. cl.   ind. cl.

i) <u>They make the garden look beautiful</u>, and <u>they attract honeybees, butterflies and hummingbirds</u>.

  prep. phr.   ind. cl.   dep. cl.

j) <u>By August</u>, <u>many of the vegetables and berries are so ripe</u> <u>that they are easy to pick and delicious to eat</u>.

18. Answers will vary. The answers below are examples only. Any independent or dependent clause that makes sense should be accepted.

a) **My friends and I walk** around the campus most evenings.

b) During spring break, **my family always travels somewhere new**.

c) **We congratulated the goalie** who played well.

d) Because I wanted to study art, **I applied to art schools in Florence and Paris**.

e) **We wandered on the forest trails all afternoon**, but eventually we found our way home.

f) She went to Florence, Italy **because she wanted to study art there**.

g) **My brother gave me some headphones** that I really liked.

h) Even though my favorite sport is volleyball, **I will also play basketball and tennis this year**.

THE SENTENCE

19. Answers will vary. The answers below are examples only.

   a) When it isn't raining, I like riding my bike after school.

   b) Whenever it snows, I can go snowboarding in Oregon.

   c) In the fall, I like taking long walks since the cool air is refreshing.

   d) When I turn sixteen years old, I'll learn to drive a car with my mother.

   e) I plan to try out for the varsity team, but first I have to improve my conditioning for more stamina.

FINAL EXERCISES

20. The two sentence fragments and one run-on are listed below with suggestions on how to correct them. Answers may vary.

   a) (fragment) Such a beautiful book. It is such a beautiful book.

   b) (run-on) He also wrote articles for *The New Yorker* magazine, some were funny, some were serious and pointed out areas where change was needed, all were well written.

   He also wrote articles for *The New Yorker* magazine. Some articles were funny, and some were serious and pointed out areas where change was needed. Nevertheless, all his articles were well written.

   c) (fragment) Like an amusing one about a mother raccoon in his backyard.

   I especially liked an amusing one about a mother raccoon in his backyard.

21. Answers will vary.

PART 5
JOBS NOUNS AND PRONOUNS DO IN SENTENCES

JOBS NOUNS AND PRONOUNS DO IN SENTENCES

1. Often there will be modifying words with the simple subject. All that together makes the complete subject.

   What are all these other words with the simple subject? They can be modifiers, phrases, or dependent clauses.

2. Answers will vary.

3. Answers will vary.

4. a) <u>Quinn and Kostya</u>, <u>looking for edible mushrooms</u>, were walking in the woods yesterday. (S, S)

   b) When they reached the pond, they saw a mysterious boy fishing on the other side. (S)

   c) They had never seen the boy before and wondered who he was. (S)

   d) Quinn thought they should walk around the pond and say hello. (S)

   e) <u>The adventurous Kostya</u> convinced her to go climb the big pine tree instead. (S)

   f) They started to walk away toward the big pine. (S)

   g) Wait! Subject = you   Did they hear something? (S)

199

JOBS NOUNS AND PRONOUNS DO IN SENTENCES

            S
h) It was the boy calling to them.

      S   S   S
i) <u>Quinn and Kostya</u> turned to wait for the boy, but he had disappeared.

    S   S
j) They quickly ran to the last spot that they had seen him but he was gone.

DIRECT OBJECTS

5. An object is the noun or pronoun that tells the goal or result of another word in a sentence. A direct object tells what the action of the verb is directed to, acted on, or resulted in. A sentence can have more than one direct object, or it can have none.

6. Answers will vary.

7. Answers will vary.

              S   D.O.
8. a) Next week I will enter my artwork in a state art show.

        S   D.O.
b) First, I must create my pottery so it has time to dry fully.

     S   D.O.
c) Next I will paint several paintings.

     S   D.O.
d) Then, I planned the design for some pen and ink drawings.

                                  S   D.O.
e) Once all the pieces of art are dry and ready, I will sign my name on each one.

       S   S
f) <u>The art show</u> is tomorrow and <u>my artwork</u> is ready.

JOBS NOUNS AND PRONOUNS DO IN SENTENCES

                          S   S   D.O.   D.O.

g) Later in the evening, <u>my friends and I</u> cleaned my art studio and made it ready for visitors.

INDIRECT OBJECTS

9. The indirect object is the noun or pronoun in a sentence that tells who or what the action of the verb is being done for.

10. Answers will vary.

11. Answers will vary.

                                                S   I.O. D.O.

12. a) On the morning of my birthday, <u>my friends</u> gave me a gift.

        S

   b) Then we celebrated with a special breakfast.

            S   I.O.   I.O. D.O.   S

   c) Later <u>my brother</u> gave my friend and me a ride to the beach so we could swim.

                        S   D.O.

   d) When we returned, <u>my favorite aunt</u> threw a surprise party for me.

        S   I.O. D.O.   D.O.

   e) <u>My friends</u> brought me cards and candy.

        S   D.O.   D.O.   D.O.

   f) We played games and music all evening and had a great time!

JOBS NOUNS AND PRONOUNS DO IN SENTENCES

THE OBJECT OF A PREPOSITION

13. The object of a preposition is the noun or pronoun that tells the goal or result of the preposition it follows.

14. Answers will vary.

15. Answers will vary.

16. Answers will vary. The prepositional phrases given below are only examples. Any prepositional phrase that makes sense and communicates well should be accepted.

                          O.P.

a) They ran **to Mr. Linden's farm**. *(add a prepositional phrase)*

                        O.P.

b) They ran **to Mr. Linden's farm** *(add a prepositional phrase)* to earn

          O.P.   O.P.

money **by taking care of the horses**. *(add a prepositional phrase)*

              O.P.

c) Early **in the morning** *(add a prepositional phrase)* they ran

      O.P.

to Mr. Linden's farm *(add a prepositional phrase)* to earn money

  O.P.   O.P.

for their trip to Asia. *(add a prepositional phrase)*

         D.O.   O.P.

d) They gave **food** *(add a direct object)* **to the horses**. *(add a prepositional phrase)*

         D.O.   O.P.

e) They gave **water** *(add a direct object)* **to the horses** *(add a prepositional phrase)*

     O.P.

in their stalls. *(add a prepositional phrase)*

JOBS NOUNS AND PRONOUNS DO IN SENTENCES

THE NOUN RESTATEMENT

17. A noun restatement is a noun or pronoun that states something again in a different way. It can restate, rename, or identify a previously stated noun or pronoun.

18. Answers will vary.

19. A subject restatement is a noun or pronoun in the sentence statement that restates, renames or more fully identifies the subject of a sentence.

20. Answers will vary.

21. a) I received a wonderful gift from my parents, the computer I wanted.

   b) My sister is learning to speak Norwegian, which is my grandparents' first language.

   c) Lewis and Clark traveled to the Pacific Ocean and one of the oldest towns in Oregon, Astoria.

   d) When they visited Beijing, they were most amazed by the Forbidden City, the former Imperial Palace of China.

22. a) The girls were looking forward to the Winter Ball, the first formal dance of the year.

   b) School dances are the best social activities we have.

   c) Some of our regular dances are the Welcome Dance and the Sweetheart's Ball.

   d) My favorite school dance is the Prom, which is held in the spring just before Commencement.

JOBS NOUNS AND PRONOUNS DO IN SENTENCES

e) Albert Einstein's parents were Hermann and Pauline Einstein.

f) Abraham Lincoln became the sixteenth U.S. President even though he was once an unknown lawyer from Illinois.

g) Some forms of Chinese art are the finest of any in the world.

h) During the Shang Dynasty in China, bronze cups and pots were crafted that were the most intricate examples of Bronze Age art in the world.

VERBS CAN ACT AS NOUNS

23. a) Horseback riding (ride) is a fantastic way to explore the countryside.

b) Should you cancel leaving (leave) today because of the snow?

c) Emmanuel refused to guess (guess) the answers to questions he didn't know.

d) We were trying to find (find) a job together.

e) Martin and Aliyah loved skiing (ski) best on tree-lined ski slopes.

f) I have wanted to play (play) football professionally for years.

FINAL EXERCISES

                   S   D.O.   O.P.

24. a) Our high school choir won first place in the state competition!

     S

b) This has never happened before.

     S   O.P.   O.P.

c) This win was the result of years of hard work.

JOBS NOUNS AND PRONOUNS DO IN SENTENCES

                S   I.O.

d) First our music director, who is an excellent musician, gave each student

       D.O.   D.O.   O.P.

an audition and chose the best singers to be in the choir.

      S   D.O.   O.P.

e) Then, he chose an assortment of music that displayed our versatility.

    O.P.   O.P.   S   I.O. D.O.

f) After months of rehearsals, the music director gave some students solos to sing.

   S   D.O.   O.P.   O.P.

g) They also practiced the reading of music for the competition.

         O.P.   O.P.   S

h) After many more rehearsals and performances, the choir was the best it had ever been.

   S   D.O. O.P.   S   D.O.

25. a) I like making all kinds of art. My brother, Giovanni, only likes computers.

   S   D.O.   D.O.

b) He can program a computer and build one.

  S   I.O. D.O.   O.P.

c) He has given me lessons on how to do simple computer programming.

       S   O.P.

d) My favorite art form is pottery, but I'm still learning about it.

JOBS NOUNS AND PRONOUNS DO IN SENTENCES

e) Eventually, I may be making fine pottery like the vases made in many
                      S   D.O
East Asian countries.
   O.P.

f) When I finish a pot now, I put my special symbol, a spiral, on the
                     S   D.O.
bottom.
 O.P.

g) I made a special pottery sculpture for my parents and gave it to them
   S   D.O.   O.P.   D.O.   O.P.
last year.

PART 6
WHAT IS CASE?

WHAT IS CASE?

1. **Case** is a grammar term that refers to the different forms a noun or pronoun takes depending on the job it is doing with other words in a sentence.

THE POSSESSIVE CASE

2. When a word shows ownership, it is in the possessive case.

3. Answers will vary.

4. Answers will vary.

5. Annika and her brother, Sven, were picking blueberries in their <u>town's</u> meadow. It was starting to get dark. Sven thought he had enough berries to make a pie, but Annika said, "Let's pick some more. I don't have enough for <u>mine</u>."

   Suddenly, they heard something crashing through the forest. <u>Sven's</u> eyes grew big when he recognized that he was looking at a bear. He tapped <u>Annika's</u> shoulder and motioned to her to be still. She froze instantly. Slowly they backed into the bushes, hoping their movements would not be detected. <u>Hers</u> were not noticed. <u>His</u> were.

THE NOMINATIVE CASE

6. When a pronoun acts as a **subject of a sentence or clause**, it is in the nominative case.

7. Answers will vary.

8. a) My brother and **I** (me, I) both play the piano.

   b) **She** (Her, She) and her friends compete at chess.

   c) **We** (Us, We), the seniors, pledge to make this the most productive school year of our lives.

   d) Who planned that event? **They** (Them, They) did.

WHAT IS CASE?

    e) Avi usually plays tennis better than **I** (I, me) do.

    f) Who wrote that play? It was **he.** (he, him).

9. a) Rafaella and ~~me~~ **I** are twins.

    b) Raoul and ~~myself~~ **I** are both on the varsity team.

    c) ~~Whom~~ **Who** did all this work? It was ~~me~~ **I**.

    d) Who is there? It is ~~her~~ **she**.

    e) Mochi writes better essays than ~~me~~ **I**.

THE OBJECTIVE CASE

10. When a word acts as an object, it is in the objective case. *As mentioned earlier, nouns don't change in the objective case, but pronouns do.*

    A pronoun will be in the objective case when it acts as a direct object, an indirect object or an object of a preposition in a sentence.

11. Answers will vary.

12. a) Is that gift for **me** (me, I)?

    b) The coach gave Hari and **him** (he, him) new basketballs to use.

    c) The teacher asked Deshaun and **her** (her, she) to start the discussion.

    d) The chess team won their tournament! It was a challenging match for **them** (they, them).

    e) It was an important milestone for **us** (we, us).

    f) I think you should give the assignment to **me** (I, me).

    g) To **whom** (Who, Whom) did you give that role in the play?

WHAT IS CASE?

    h) Do you know who can unlock the cabinet for **us** (we, us)?

    i) My father gave my brother and **me** (I, me) spending money.

    j) **Whom** (Who, Whom) is the special dinner for?

13. a) The candy is for ~~myself~~. **me**

    b) Our grandmother gave Mateo and ~~I~~ **me** our gifts early.

    c) Abeni and Abeo are sisters from Nigeria who are coming to visit ~~we~~ **us**.

    d) The best soccer player will be ~~he~~ **him**.

    e) People were waiting at the food bank until food could be served to ~~they~~ **them**.

    f) For ~~who~~ **whom** are you waiting?

14. Answers will vary. Below are sample answers.

    a) The boys and **I** are going snowboarding.

    b) I saw **them** over by the baseball field.

    c) It was **I** who decorated the room.

    d) You and **I** can do it by ourselves.

    e) The job was given to **him** and **me**.

    f) **She** and her sister were here yesterday.

    g) **Who** is coming to dinner?

    h) I can't wait to see Amol **whom** I haven't seen in a year.

    i) **We** students are happy with the schedule change.

    j) The teachers gave awards to those of **us** who worked hard all month.

WHAT IS CASE?

FINAL EXERCISE

15. a) My sister and ~~her~~ **she** both took violin lessons.

    b) Mikhail and ~~myself~~ **I** will be happy to explain that.

    c) The bus driver picked up Larissa and ~~she~~ **me**.

    d) All of us students researched that current event.

    e) Who would lend my roommate and ~~I~~ **me** a dollar?

    f) The students' video had a section about Manuel and me.

    g) The children's room was decorated for their birthday.

    h) Both Pierre and ~~him~~ **he** were given parts in the play.

    i) My mother made dinner for my friends and ~~I~~ **me**.

    j) ~~Whom~~ **Who** is doing the cover artwork?

    k) It was ~~me~~ **I**.

    l) My grandfather is the one person for ~~who~~ **whom** I would change my schedule.

www.ingramcontent.com/pod-product-compliance
Lightning Source LLC
Chambersburg PA
CBHW080440170426
43195CB00017B/2835